TIPS FOR CONTAINER GARDENING

TIPS FOR CONTAINER GARDENING

300 GREAT IDEAS FOR GROWING FLOWERS, VEGETABLES & HERBS

EDITORS & CONTRIBUTORS OF
Fine Gardening

The Taunton Press

The Taunton Press, Inc., 63 South Main Street, PO Box 5506, Newtown, CT 06470-5506
e-mail: tp@taunton.com

Editor: Jennifer Renjilian Morris
Copy editor: Valerie Cimino
Indexer: Jay Kreider
Jacket/cover and interior design: Rita Sowins / Sowins Design
Layout: Rita Sowins / Sowins Design

Fine Gardening® is a trademark of The Taunton Press, Inc., registered in the U.S. Patent and Trademark Office.

Library of Congress Cataloging-in-Publication Data
Tips for container gardening : 300 great ideas for growing flowers, vegetables, and herbs / editors and contributors
of Fine Gardening ; [editor: Jennifer Renjilian Morris].
    p. cm.
 ISBN 978-1-60085-340-1
 1. Container gardening. 2. Gardens--Design. 3. Plants, Potted. I. Morris, Jennifer Renjilian.
 SB418.T57 2011
 635.9'86--dc22

                    2010047878

Printed in the United States of America
10 9 8 7 6 5 4 3 2 1

The following manufacturers/names appearing in *Tips for Container Gardening* are trademarks: Babylon®,
Bandana®, Belleza™, Bonfire®, Cabana®, Catalina®, Compact Innocence®, Dragon Wing®, Dream Catcher™, Festival
Grass™, King Tut®, Lemon Swirl®, Matrix™, Molimba®, Napoleon™, Senorita Rosalita®, Soprano®, Starla™, Summer
Wave®, Sundew Springs™, Superbells®, Supertunia®, Sweet Caroline®, Tiger Eyes™, Ups-A-Daisy®, Zinfandel™.

CONTENTS

INTRODUCTION   2

DESIGN   4
Design Principles   6
In the Landscape   23
Matching the Pot to the Plant or Place   30
Color   41
Foliage   51
Designs for the Seasons   64
Choosing Plants   77
Edibles   79
Drought-Tolerant Plants   90
Water Gardens   95

POTS & PLANTERS   100
Pick a Pot   102
Not Your Typical Containers   110
Window Boxes   118
Hanging Baskets   128
Care   136

PLANTING & MAINTENANCE   142
Soil   144
Potting   156
Watering   169
Pruning   179
Pests & Other Problems   187
Overwintering   190

USDA HARDINESS ZONE MAP   198
CONTRIBUTORS   199
CREDITS   200
INDEX   201

Introduction

CONTAINERS ARE THE GREAT GARDEN EQUALIZER. No matter where you live, how big your space, or how small your budget, you can do it. Of course, attempting to grow plants in the artificial environment of a pot presents challenges. These challenges are not new, and other container gardeners out there have struggled with them too—and succeeded. And if gardeners like to do anything (other than complain about the deer or the weather), it is to share a success story.

That is what the tips in this book are—gardeners from around the country telling you what worked for them. You will hear about ways to reduce watering, improve drainage, and eliminate chores. The tips also tell you how to grow specific plants and which varieties work well together. Think of it as an entire family offering you the advice you need (except in this case, it is easier to ignore it if you want to).

One tip that is not in this book might be something you already know: Once you start gardening in containers, it can be difficult to stop. You will find yourself growing all kinds of plants you wouldn't have normally. A tropical from the Brazilian rainforest? Sure, just bring it inside for the winter. A redwood tree? Make it into a bonsai. You will contemplate turning any random object into a home for plants. An old tuba could work. So could those shoes your son outgrew. Pots can become a passion. And when it does, and others start asking you how you do it, remember to share all these tips that helped you become a successful container gardener.

—Steve Aitken, *Fine Gardening* editor

DESIGN

Design Principles	6
In the Landscape	23
Matching the Pot to the Plant or Place	30
Color	41
Foliage	51
Designs for the Seasons	64
Choosing Plants	77
Edibles	79
Drought-Tolerant Plants	90
Water Gardens	95

Design Principles

1 Soprano® Purple African Daisy   2 Pansy   3 'Ogon' Japanese sweet flag   4 'Goldilocks' creeping Jenny

RULE OF THREE

Three or four plants are all it takes to make a great combo. Using the classic rule of three—a thriller, a filler, and a spiller—is still the safest and most popular recipe for successful mixes. In the photo above, colorful, cool mounds of pansy and African daisy are separated and enlivened with spiky sweet flag. 'Goldilocks' creeping Jenny adds a final touch of bright color spilling over the container's rim.

Rita Randolph, Jackson, Tennessee

MULTIPLE POTS JAZZ IT UP

I have adapted the thriller-filler-spiller container recipe to container clusters. The technique calls for using a large, eye-catching thriller as the centerpiece, adding billowy mounding plants as fillers around it, and finishing with a cascading spiller that tumbles out and softens the edges of the arrangement. I put a thriller in one pot, some fillers in others, and spillers in still more; I then group them, tweaking the design until it looks perfect. The result is instant impact: an impressive display of well-grown plants in attractive pots.

Steve Silk, Farmington, Connecticut

1 Bandana® Trailing Gold lantana   2 Zinfandel™ oxalis   3 'Patriot Tangerine' lantana   4 'Torbay Dazzler' giant dracaena

TRADITION, WITH A TWIST

I've learned to appreciate container designs that give a nod to history—but with a twist. For example, why not pair a variegated version of the traditional green spike with a punch lantana and some oxalis in place of geraniums and vinca vine? It's classic but fun.

Scott Endres, Minneapolis, Minnesota

1 'Red Rooster' leatherleaf sedge   2 'Black Pearl' ornamental pepper   3 Dinosaur kale   4 Belleza™ Dark
Pink gaura   5 Starla™ Appleblossom pentas   6 'Bourbon Street' copperleaf   7 'Redskin' dwarf dahlia
8 'Caramel' heuchera   9 Jasmine   10 'Brown Sugar Drop' coleus

MAKE RELIABLE PERENNIALS THE BACKBONE

Here's a trick to eliminate the worry of trying new plants: Sprinkle in trial plants with
perennials you know will thrive and that have similar color, form, and texture. If a new
test plant fails, just remove it, and let the remaining reliable, low-maintenance plants
fill in the gaps.

Scott Endres, Minneapolis, Minnesota

COPY GOOD IDEAS

If you don't know what to do or you're afraid to try something new, do what professionals like me do: plagiarize. My cell-phone camera is full of photos of pots I plan on copying. I snap a photo anytime I see something that I like, then when I'm planning my pots, I always have somewhere to start.

Jimmy Turner, Dallas, Texas

A FORMULA FOR HEIGHT-TO-WIDTH PROPORTION

To be visually pleasing to our eyes, the height of the plants in a container should be, in general, one-and-a half to two times the height of a container. If the container happens to be wider than it is tall, then the plant heights should be one-and-a-half to two times the diameter of the container.

Scott Endres, Minneapolis, Minnesota

FILL YOUR POT TO THE BRIM

Visitors to my greenhouse often ask me how many plants they can safely put in a pot. The answer depends on how much money you have. In all seriousness, plants grow until they touch and mingle anyway, so filling a pot is quite acceptable. Just make sure that all the plants have compatible growing habits so that one eager grower won't take over the others. You can usually find this information on a plant tag, but be sure to ask questions at the nursery if you're picking a plant that doesn't include growing requirements.

Rita Randolph, Jackson, Tennessee

DON'T BE AFRAID OF CHANGE

Don't be afraid to change things around mid-season. If something isn't living up to your expectations, take it out. I use a bread knife to cut through the roots around the plant, and then I pull it out and add a new plant if the design needs it.

Deanne Fortnam, Nashua, New Hampshire

A LITTLE HEIGHT CAN MAKE ALL THE DIFFERENCE

A focal point doesn't have to be large to grab attention; it just needs to be in the right spot. A simple combo wouldn't have the same impact down among the rest of the plants, but it easily commands attention atop a decorative pillar or pedestal. A pillar with pale tones will not divert too much attention from the surroundings.

Brandi Spade, Newtown, Connecticut

1 Miniature pine tree   2 'Silver Gray' kalanchoe   3 Blue echeveria   4 Variegated elephant bush   5 Baby jade
6 'Silver Spoons' echeveria

BRING SMALL DETAILS INTO VIEW

Elevating containers keeps them from becoming a tripping hazard and brings the plants up high enough for visitors to be able to appreciate the details of a miniature landscape. These same details might easily be lost if placed at ground level.

Scott Endres, Minneapolis, Minnesota

A TRIANGLE ALWAYS WORKS

Containers can be grouped into vignettes the same way plants can. A triangular arrangement of pots will produce quick, pleasing results. In design terms, a triangle consists of a dominant central element flanked by components of smaller stature. This form is a staple of all art forms for good reason: It always works. The colorful hibiscus (see photo above) serves as the apex of a triangular composition completed by subordinate elements placed slightly in front and to the side.

Sydney Eddison, Newtown, Connecticut

ALLOW ONE POT TO DOMINATE

A container grouping will quickly fall into place if the tallest element is placed at the rear of the composition, with the other pots on either side. Plant the tall container with something appropriately commanding so that it will dominate the grouping. If you have two containers of similar stature, raise one on a pedestal to give it prominence.

Sydney Eddison, Newtown, Connecticut

HIGH-PROFILE CONTAINERS

For front-and-center locations like your front entry, choose some free-flowing annuals or colorful foliage so that you always have a punch of interest, no matter what the season. Evergreens are also a good choice. They're steady and dependable and always look good.

Michelle Gervais, New Milford, Connecticut

1 Red alternanthera   2 Lemon Swirl® lantana
3 Red chicken gizzard iresine   4 'Vancouver Centennial'
geranium   5 Creeping wire vine   6 Variegated ground ivy
7 Napoleon™ papyrus   8 'Freckles' coleus   9 'Tangletown's
Dark Secret' coleus

REPEATING PLANTS CREATES
CONSISTENT HARMONY

By repeating plants, pots, and colors, you have the option to mix things up a little,
knowing that there is a solid framework as a base. In the photo on the left, a common
green container color echoes throughout the group. Further repetition occurs with
the reappearance of similar plants and color patterns.

Scott Endres, Minneapolis, Minnesota

1 'Inky Fingers' coleus   2 'Red Sensation' cordyline   3 'Oehme' variegated palm sedge   4 'Colchester White' dusty miller

CONTRAST AND CONNECT WITH OTHER PLANTS

Color usually makes the first impression and often dominates in a composition, but don't forget the importance of its interplay with line, form, and texture. Line leads the eye from one area to another and ties a planting together—for instance, when a plant seems to explode upward and outward, drawing the eye in those directions. Form gives a sense of placement in space and can also suggest feeling, like the strength of a triangular shape or the comfort of a smooth, rounded sphere. Texture is the perception of coarseness or fineness and the variation in both dimension and tactile feeling. Big plants with a few big spaces between them appear coarse, whereas smaller, more linear parts, like those of a fern, denote a fine texture. Coleus abundantly provide all four design elements and so make excellent choices for memorable container plantings. For example, a gently curving mass of coarser coleus contrasts sharply with distinctively linear, more open, finer companions (see the photo above).

Ray Rogers, North Brunswick, New Jersey

SHAPES WORK TOGETHER

The easiest way to look at shape is to think of the contour created by each plant's silhouette within your container. As with many principles of plant pairing, opposites make great companions: Upright shapes pair well with mounding shapes, and mounding shapes are good next to trailing shapes.

Scott Endres, Minneapolis, Minnesota

1 King Tut® papyrus   2 Bauer's dracaena   3 Purple heart   4 Superbells® Dreamsicle calibrachoa   5 Golden creeping Jenny

STRONG VERTICAL LINES ADD IMPORT

Psychologically, a heavy vertical line gives the design an overall feeling of strength. It can also give the impression that the arrangement is taller.

Scott Endres, Minneapolis, Minnesota

PROPORTION DETERMINES THE NUMBER OF POTS IN A CLUSTER

I look to nearby architectural elements or plant masses to provide cues for how big to make the cluster, often thinking in thirds—a proportion that is naturally pleasing to the eye. The size of a container cluster, for example, might be three times as tall and wide as the path it frames. Or it might be two-thirds the size of a nearby wall, small tree, or shrub.

Steve Silk, Farmington, Connecticut

GET MORE STRUCTURE IN THE GARDEN

When you have a lot of plants in your garden, you need to add definition to the chaos. One way to do this is to place pots right into the beds. Containers add a structural element to the plantings and break things up visually.

Jennie Hammill, Seattle, Washington

SELECTING PERENNIALS

Pick a perennial that will be the dominant center, then choose at least two others with foliage and flowers that contrast or blend with your primary plant.

Christine Froelich, Sodus Point, New York

KEEP 'EM CLOSE

When you choose the location for your edibles, consider more than just sun and shade. You also want the pots to have easy access to water and harvesting. And keep the pots close to your kitchen so that you won't have to trek out to the garden for a few leaves of basil or lettuce for tonight's salad.

Fine Gardening editors

A SIMPLE TEEPEE FOR VINES

If you're growing vines in your container, you'll need to support them. The easiest way to do that is to buy colorful trellises that look like teepees that vines grow up. Or you can easily make your own bamboo teepee by arranging three or four stakes together and tying them at the top.

Fine Gardening editors

BEYOND PLANTS

Don't be afraid to add inanimate objects to your plantings. Try painted bamboo stakes, tomato spirals, gazing balls, and anything else that strikes your fancy. Your options are endless, but be sure to choose something that matches your style.

Fine Gardening editors

In the Landscape

ROOFTOP SUCCESS

When selecting plants for a rooftop space, be sure that the plants and combinations not only work up close but also fit the large scale of city views without interfering with them. Bold use of color, contrast, and repetition helps achieve these goals without skimping on diversity. And don't forget to choose plants that can endure the wind exposure of a rooftop location.

Scott Endres, Minneapolis, Minnesota

1 Golden Italian cypress   2 'Mystic Illusion' dahlia   3 Purple heart   4 Festival Grass™ cordyline   5 Dinosaur kale

SHOW OFF FRONT ENTRIES

Front-entry containers require special attention to the scale and style of your home, the distance from which the containers are first seen, and the scale of the neighborhood. Generally, this means planting in large containers, using plants that provide bold brushstrokes with pronounced focal points, and ensuring a clear contrast between ingredients to command attention even from a distance. The details are still important, though. Keep in mind that your containers are designed not only for the up-close views of you and your guests but also for passersby, like drivers and pedestrians.

Scott Endres, Minneapolis, Minnesota

BEYOND THE TRADITIONAL ENTRY DESIGN

Too often we think we need two identical planters—on each side of the doorway—to create a successful entry planting. Planters can be single, clustered, freestanding, or attached to the house as window boxes to complement an entry.

Scott Endres, Minneapolis, Minnesota

TRANSFORM A SEATING AREA

When designing containers for seating areas, rely less on bold, dramatic brushstrokes and instead take advantage of subtle plant details that would be lost in other situations. And remember that containers function as more than just art; they are useful elements for both creating privacy and screening unwanted views.

Scott Endres, Minneapolis, Minnesota

A PRIVATE OASIS

Large planters add a sense of enclosure to an open deck while providing a view from other parts of the backyard.

Scott Endres, Minneapolis, Minnesota

DRESS UP THE POOL WITH POTS

Incorporating container plants around the swimming pool boosts the sculptural element and incorporates opportunities for seasonal color. Arrange odd numbers of pots in clusters, or use three identical containers in a row as a striking focal point. Have fun with the character of your containers, but stay true to the style of your home.

Stephen Gabor, Venice, California

ADD DEPTH TO BORDERS

Pots help soften the boundaries of my property. By placing the containers a bit forward rather than tucked up against the back fence or the sides of the house, I am able to add depth, which makes the "walls" seem farther away. This helps me feel like the borders of my lot are disappearing.

Jennie Hammill, Seattle, Washington

AN HERB "GARDEN"

By planting herbs of one type in a single container, I have the fun of arranging—and rearranging—them to create a pleasing garden scene. If I don't like the effect, there's no need to rip out plants: I just move the containers around. And when plants like nasturtiums finish blooming, I can move them to the back of the "garden" and bring others forward.

Jo Ann Gardner, Westport, New York

1 Rough bark maple   2 'Aureola' Japanese forest grass   3 Perennial impatiens   4 Japanese blood grass   5 'Crow Feather' foam flower   6 'Regal Splendor' hosta   7 Himalayan maidenhair fern

INSPIRED BY THE FOREST

To feel natural, the plants in woodland designs should mimic a forest environment. Try an understory of herbaceous and evergreen perennials suited for dappled light. The delicate texture of grasses and ferns contrasts with bolder leaves of hosta and foam flower. Soft yellow tones can add some light.

Karen Chapman, Seattle, Washington

USE BIG PLANTS FOR BIG SPACES

Large, simple container plantings are a must in a wooded setting to maintain a balance with mature trees. One container may not be enough, but two can achieve the impact necessary for the scale of the open space that surrounds them.

Scott Endres, Minneapolis, Minnesota

Matching the Pot to the Plant or Place

PLANTS SHOULD COMPLEMENT THE POT

When designing a pot that will have only one type of plant in it, it's important to pair the size and proportion of a plant with a complementary pot. In general, plants with a rounded habit are successfully paired with pots of low, chubby proportions. Blue anise sage, a plant that attracts hummingbirds, has an overall rounded form that looks stunning in a squat pot. The vertical effect of a larger, more upright pot can be enhanced by pairing it with a similarly shaped plant, such as a tropical smoke bush, cannas, upright coleus, or grasses. Top a small, narrow pot with a spiky hat by choosing a plant such as fiber optic grass or an agave (*Agave*s pp. and cvs.). The same look can be achieved with a larger narrow pot using a fountain grass. Ornate flaring urns benefit from the blowsy habit of shrubs such as hydrangeas or flowering maples, which add Victorian charm to a cottage-garden setting.

June Hutson, Missouri

1 'Angelina' sedum   2 Blue echeveria   3 'Cape Blanco' spoon-leaved sedum   4 'Kiwi' aeonium
5 Tree aeonium   6 Blue chalk sticks

MAKE IT FIT THE LOCATION

Don't think about just the container when you choose plants; also think about where you're putting the container. Choose plants that echo the colors and patterns in the container, but also consider matching them to the display area. In the photo above, the 'Kiwi' aeonium pairs well with both the container and the table on which it sits, creating a warm, sunny effect.

Linda Roark, Palo Alto, California

LET THE CONTAINER GIVE YOU A CLUE

Matching your pot color to your plants doesn't apply only to flowers. A pot's color can inspire your choice of edible-plant colors as well. For example, a burgundy pot (see the photo at right) lends itself to plants like red-stemmed chard, scarlet-flowered nasturtiums, and an assortment of purple foliage to highlight its rich color.

Danielle Sherry, Niantic, Connecticut

COLOR MATTERS

Be careful with colorful containers because more is not necessarily better. Too much color can be distracting. A good rule of thumb is to make sure the containers would look good together even if they were empty.

Steve Silk, Farmington, Connecticut

1 Alpine strawberry   2 'Rainbow Mix' chard   3 'Empress of India' nasturtium   4 Chocolate mint   5 'Purple Ruffles' basil
6 Purple ornamental cabbage   7 'Calabrese' broccoli

1 'Chapel Hill Gold' lantana   2 Variegated boxwood   3 'Silvery Sunproof' liriope   4 Sundew Springs™ lysimachia

CONTAINERS CAN BE FOCAL POINTS

Don't cover up attractive or decorative containers with a lot of pendulous plants—or else you'll never see the pot. You can add one or two trailers for extra eye appeal, if you can keep them under control and clip them back from time to time.

Rita Randolph, Jackson, Tennessee

STYLISH FORMAL CONTAINERS

For formal containers (which can include contemporary and traditional designs), success depends upon a careful marriage of pot and plants. A sophisticated style calls for restraint in color, embellishment, and plants. The vessel itself has a strong presence and is as important as the contents. The best combinations focus on foliage and texture, because blossoms are often fleeting.

Karen Chapman, Seattle, Washington

DON'T GET TOO FANCY

Do not use a container that is too ornate. You want your plants, not the pot, to be the focal point of your display. An ornate container will distract you and draw attention away from the plant. If you choose a container that has a lot of ornamentation, use it as a display piece by itself and not as a container for plants.

Linda Roark, Palo Alto, California

BIG HOUSE, BIG CONTAINERS

A big house requires a big pot, not a mini combo. Avoid pots that are too small for the scale of their environment (or too large if you're working in a small space, like a narrow walkway). Visualize your container from where it will be viewed, and compare it to the scale of your home. Containers will often look a lot bigger on a cart at the garden center than they will in front of your home, so don't be intimidated by size. Nothing looks sillier than a couple of puny pots sitting outside even a modest-size home.

Scott Endres, Minneapolis, Minnesota

TABLETOP STUNNERS

Selecting plants for a tabletop container can be frustrating: If, for example, the plants grow too tall, the container often has to be set to one side as people sit down to talk. Dwarf or slow-growing plants are, therefore, the way to go. Containers can be small, alpine-looking troughs or naturalistic combinations.

Rita Randolph, Jackson, Tennessee

1 'Lady in Red' fern   2 Variegated roof iris   3 'Silver Jewel' begonia   4 'Fantasia' variegated English ivy

UNIQUE POTS CALL FOR SIMPLICITY

Specialized pots create an opportunity for unique combos. Some of the newest and most popular containers available are made to look aged and are often molded into the shapes of tree trunks, logs, and branches. Unique containers don't need a lot of fussy plants. The simplest approach is sometimes the most effective. Try filling a faux-bois (false-wood) container with iris, fern, and begonia to keep that natural woodsy feel.

Rita Randolph, Jackson, Tennessee

1 'Touch of Class' Jacob's ladder   2 'Icicles' helichrysum   3 'Cape Blanco' sedum   4 'Zwartkop' aeonium   5 'Tricolor' sedum

ICY PLANTS COOL DOWN WARM-COLORED POTS

Metallic containers can look cold or hot, depending on the metal and on how you use them. Turn down the thermostat of a bronzed container using cool silver succulents and deep black aeonium.

Michelle Gervais, New Milford, Connecticut

BREAK THE RULES ON POT COLOR

Designers often tell you to stick to just one pot color in a small space, but this is something I have failed at miserably. Instead, I group my containers somewhat by color or in close proximity to a piece of architecture with a similar hue. My red pots, for example, echo the color of some nearby French doors.

Jennie Hammill, Seattle, Washington

BOLD PLANTS NEED A BIG POT 〉

A half whiskey barrel provides enough space to plant large vegetables, including dinosaur kale and hot peppers. Big vegetable varieties give a container a big visual impact. A large pot also makes it possible to squeeze in not just one but several bold stars.

Danielle Sherry, Niantic, Connecticut

1 'Juliet' grape tomato   2 Dinosaur kale   3 Nasturtium
4 'Petit Marseillais' pepper   5 'Black Pearl' pepper

CORRAL FLOPPED SEDUMS IN A POT

In late summer, my tall sedums always flop over. One year, I dug up a flopped clump of 'Autumn Joy' and plopped it into a tall, narrow pot to transport it to a new spot. Because I didn't know where I wanted to put it, I added a little potting soil around the root ball and set it aside. A few weeks later, the sedum looked stunning growing out of the top of the pot, so I left it in the pot and placed it back in the garden. I realized that this was a great way to corral sedums and prevent them from flopping: The pot acts like a growth ring to keep the plants upright. Pots that are taller than they are wide work best, and they should be approximately the height of the sedum you want to control.

Cookie Trivett, Millfield, Ohio

DON'T DETRACT FROM YOUR COLOR SCHEME

The safest choice for a color-themed design is one with a neutral tone, like that of concrete or cast limestone, because it will work with whatever plant color you use. Terra-cotta is great, but remember that it is actually orange-hued, so you'll have to plan for that when choosing your plant colors. If, for example, your intention is to create a soft, frothy blue arrangement and you plant it in a terra-cotta container, the orange color of the pot is about as far away as you can get from blue, so the overall effect of the design might not be what you want. If you'd like a bit more excitement in your arrangements, you can choose a strong-colored container for your designs, but bear in mind that the color of the pot needs to enhance—rather than detract from—the overall effect of the composition.

Deanne Fortnam, Nashua, New Hampshire

LIGHT UP THE NIGHT

Add white flowers to containers whenever possible, because they are the ones you'll notice at night.

Kimberly Crane, Charleston, South Carolina

Dusty miller

HIGHLIGHT WITH SILVER AND GOLD

Silver and gold foliage are fantastic in their ability to make a container combination shine, especially in entry combinations that need help emphasizing details from a distance. Silver plants will make blues and purples look a bit bluer, and gold foliage will offer a little warmth to cool-color schemes. Both read well from a distance and, just like a highlighter, bring attention to important parts of a design, often acting as a backdrop for a dramatic dark leaf or adding emphasis to a container's edge. Whatever the use, silver and gold plants are important tools for maximizing a container design's potential.

Scott Endres, Minneapolis, Minnesota

LESS IS MORE WHEN IT COMES TO COLOR

The combinations we generally like have a pleasing harmony or contrast. Pay attention to intensity, avoiding the combination of too many different pale pastels and saturated pure hues, which can make a combination look chaotic. Likewise, don't mix together too many different warm and cool colors. Stick with two or three—maybe four—agreeable colors.

Rita Randolph, Jackson, Tennessee

AVOID A COLOR POTPOURRI

Colors must be chosen carefully, as if you were decorating your living room or picking out an outfit. I see lots of containers with dreadful color combinations, in which it looks like the gardener just went with one of each color. Pick a color scheme based on what surrounds the container, and stick to it. And avoid placing dark plants with red undertones next to dark plants with purple undertones. Don't pair blue-silvers with green-silvers either.

Flora Grubb, San Francisco, California

'SILVER FALLS' SHIMMERS LIKE A WATERFALL

'Silver Falls' dichondra is like the Crystal Gayle of the plant world (well, perhaps after Crystal has gone gray). Strands of small, fuzzy, coinlike leaves cascade like a silver waterfall. In a hanging basket, it can keep going straight down for several feet, creating a curtain you can't help but touch. It's an easy, fast-growing, undemanding plant that you can find inexpensively at most nurseries.

Michelle Gervais, New Milford, Connecticut

1 'Gold Dust' croton   2 'Sturrocks Veitchii' croton   3 'Orange Marmalade' firecracker flower   4 Golden trailing spike moss

A SPLASH OF CITRUS COLOR

Crotons are valuable container elements because they lend splashy color and tropical resilience
to combinations in full sun or partial shade.

Jill Schroer, St. Charles, Missouri

AN EXPLOSION OF COLOR

Bonfire® begonia is a sizzling-hot little number —a must-buy for its intense color and sultry pizzazz. It is best grown in a container, where it will flaunt its fiery orange-red flowers all summer long as it flows over the edges. Keep it well-watered and fertilize monthly. You'll never regret a cent spent on this stunner.

Rizaniño "Riz" Reyes, Shoreline, Washington

A COLOR REACTION

All colors evoke a reaction from the viewer. Cooler colors, like blues and violets, are soothing and evoke a sense of calmness, while warm colors, like reds and oranges, grab people's attention and emphasize those areas of the design.

Scott Endres, Minneapolis, Minnesota

'Sedona' coleus

COLEUS LIVEN UP HARD-TO-REACH AREAS

Coleus can—and should—be used as the exclamation point in a container. Their seductive color spectrum ranges from bright chartreuse to nearly pitch-black. They can offer a deeper saturation of the colors found in a surrounding border and will work hard to bring attention away from the harsh edges of lifeless patios and walkways. I often include a specific variety in my containers and then repeat the same variety in a nearby section of border to tie the spaces together.

Scott Endres, Minneapolis, Minnesota

PURPLEHEART IS AN OLD-FASHIONED GEM

Purpleheart is a beloved, ancient house-plant that really shines as a container player. The dusky matte purple stems and strappy leaves are coarse and striking and are the perfect foil for finer green foliage and pink or yellow flowers. As a matter of fact, purpleheart has pink flowers along the stems amid the foliage—a charming bonus. At the end of the season, dig up this plant and bring it inside, or take cuttings, which root in the blink of an eye in a glass of water on the windowsill.

Michelle Gervais, New Milford, Connecticut

VARIEGATED POTATO VINE PACKS A GOLDEN PUNCH

The golden leaf margins on this perennial vine are the perfect companion to hot-colored annuals such as verbenas and red petunias. This is a dense plant that forms a significant mass in a container. In fall, the starry white to pale blue flowers are replaced by shiny black fruit. In warm climates, it might be evergreen.

Michelle Gervais, New Milford, Connecticut

PARROT'S BEAK STRADDLES BOTH SIDES OF THE COLOR WHEEL

The finely textured, gray-green foliage of parrot's beak is like a frothy skirt of tulle for your container. It begs to be paired with blues, purples, and rosy reds, but be careful: Starting in midsummer, the cool foliage occasionally sports beaklike orange to scarlet flowers (see inset photo), which can throw your carefully planned cool color scheme for a loop. This one takes some experimenting with to use successfully, but it's worth the effort.

Fine Gardening editors

1 'Clemson Spineless' okra   2 'Early Jersey Wakefield' cabbage   3 'Tricolor' sage   4 'Banana Split' nasturtium   5 Matrix™ Yellow pansy   6 Curly parsley   7 Thai basil   8 Tomatillo

A SIMPLE COLOR PALETTE FOR EDIBLES

If the thought of bright orange peppers and hot red tomatoes makes you cringe, try using vegetables with softer hues. You can do a container with mostly greens and yellows, and it doesn't have to be boring. Try yellow-flowered companions like 'Banana Split' nasturtium and Matrix™ Yellow pansy. A splash of a complementary color, like purple, breaks up the color monotony, while fleshy leaves of cabbage can add some textural interest.

Danielle Sherry, Niantic, Connecticut

Foliage

EDIBLE AND BEAUTIFUL

Bold foliage is always a good addition to containers. To add more than just foliage, though, use kale or curly parsley to add great texture and something tasty.

Fine Gardening editors

DON'T FORGET TEXTURE AS AN ELEMENT

When mixing and matching plants, keep their textures in mind. A blend of glossy, matte, and/or fuzzy leaves adds another level of interest, as does combining fine, broad, rounded, and/or jagged foliage. I like to use contrasting texture to create dramatic container plantings. The key is to choose a variety of textures. Too much of one texture, such as large, chunky leaves, is like trying to put together colorful pieces of a jigsaw puzzle that don't quite match up. In this case you can find the connecting pieces in the form of fine-textured plants.

Rita Randolph, Jackson, Tennessee

1 'Occold Shield' geranium   2 'Sedona' coleus   3 Persian shiled   4 Tiger Eyes™ cutleaf staghorn sumac
5 'Watermelon' coleus   6 'Burgundy Threadleaf' alternanthera

ADD DRAMA

Simply stated, the greater the contrast in texture, the more dramatic the plant combination will be. Coarse-textured plants, which demand attention with their dramatic foliage, and fine-textured plants, with their seductive, touch-me qualities, make perfect companions. The soft, fine textures make the coarse textures appear more dramatic, while the coarse textures enhance the fine-textured qualities—a perfect partnership. Or try fine-textured foliage placed against bigger leaves and dark foliage next to brighter leaves. The contrast makes each plant's characteristics more pronounced.

Scott Endres, Minneapolis, Minnesota

HOLDING IT ALL TOGETHER

Soft, tiny, or ferny foliage interspersed among large, dominant leaves is the glue that holds all the foliage together. Whether you use the thriller-filler-spiller design technique, the planting-in-odd-numbers technique, or the color-theory approach, your main focus should be on using complementary textures. That will make it easy to create exciting container combinations—even if they're simply green.

Rita Randolph, Jackson, Tennessee

1 Dream Catcher™ beautybush   2 Pentas   3 'Red Hot Rio' coleus   4 Elephant's ear   5 Coleus

GOLDEN FOLIAGE GLOWS WITH RICH APPEAL

Shrubs with gold-tinted foliage have year-round appeal. They add a touch of bright-ness to any combo. I use these colorful bushes in containers for a year or two before they grow too large and need to be moved to the garden. In the mix shown above, the frost-hardy foliage of Dream Catcher™ beautybush spills out beneath some of my favorite annuals and perennials. As the cool days progress, the foliage will turn from lime tinted with gold to a deep shade of gold with hints of orange.

Rita Randolph, Jackson, Tennessee

SILVER FOLIAGE CATCHES THE EYE

Striking begonia leaves will last longer than any blooms, so they are perfect for building a combination around.

Rita Randolph, Jackson, Tennessee

NOT ENOUGH SUN FOR SUCCULENTS?

Succulents are easy to grow but need the sun to thrive. No sun? Maybe succulents are best admired in someone else's container. To create textural wonderlands in the shade, try foliage-forward small hostas (photo 1), club mosses (photo 2), and baby tears (photo 3). These shady characters will be right at home in your containers and offer similar results.

Scott Endres, Minneapolis, Minnesota

SOFT, THREADLIKE LEAVES FOR THREE SEASONS

'Icicles' Helichrysum—an upright, bushy form of helichrysum—is a fantastic foil for other foliage in a container. Because of its remarkable tolerance of cold and heat, 'Icicles' will look good for three, and sometimes four, seasons. This makes it a no-brainer for my pots every year.

Scott Endres, Minneapolis, Minnesota

A BANANA THAT FITS

I like to use 'Siam Ruby' banana in my containers because it doesn't seem to be as vigorous as other bananas, leaving room for complementary plants.

Rita Randolph, Jackson, Tennessee

BIG LEAVES, BIG IMPACT

If you need to create impact in a big space, look no further than red Abyssinian banana. This tropical giant adds the instant size and drama that large containers need and is easy to grow. This plant grows quickly in the heat of summer, so even a plant that starts off small at the beginning of the season will produce big results.

Scott Endres, Minneapolis, Minnesota

GRASS MAKES A STRONG STATEMENT

Sometimes impact can be established with clear vertical lines that give a sense of strength to a combo. Upright grasses are the perfect solution, and one of my favorites is miscanthus. From day one, its fine-textured, outward-arching blades bring elegance and refinement to an arrangement. I leave it in through the fall, and sometimes winter, as it usually develops nice color as it dries.

Scott Endres, Minneapolis, Minnesota

1 'Princess' napier grass   2 'Alabama Sunset' coleus   3 Golden shrimp plant   4 'Sedona' coleus   5 'Sweet Caroline Bewitched Purple' sweet potato vine   6 Himalayan honeysuckle

TALL GRASS ELEVATES A COMBO

'Princess' napier grass can reach 4 ft. tall, as high as some dwarf bananas. It makes a wonderful vertical statement. The vertical structure will stay tall and strong because 'Princess' does not flop like other grasses.

Rita Randolph, Jackson, Tennessee

TOP CHOICE FOR SHADE

I don't know of any better group of plants for my shady mixes than mosses. They're the ultimate in lush foliage, fine texture, and classic good looks. The blue tone of peacock spike moss simply glows when combined with green foliage.

Rita Randolph, Jackson, Tennessee

SOFTEN THE LOOK

Blue fescue's fine foliage has a wonderful hue and slender blades that soften the edges of other plants. Their compact growth will continue to expand until their leaf tips flow over the container rim.

Rita Randolph, Jackson, Tennessee

INSTANT COLOR

Plants with bright foliage offer immediate focus in mixed containers while letting their neighbors fill in over time.

Scott Endres, Minneapolis, Minnesota

COLORFUL SPILLER

'Prairie Fire' is an easy-to-grow evergreen that's native to New Zealand. It has brilliant red and orange foliage in the fall, which sets it apart from other native grasses. The narrow bronze and green foliage during the warmer months adds grace to a container as a spiller.

Dee Nash, Guthrie, Oklahoma

TREES IN POTS

Choose a tree that is naturally small at maturity, is in excellent health, is at least one zone hardier than yours, and has been container grown all its life. Citrus trees, dwarf Japanese maples (*Acer palmatum* cvs., Zones 6–8) and dwarf Canadian hemlocks (*Tsuga Canadensis* cvs., Zones 4–8), are among our favorites, and all do well in the partial shade that most of us prefer for our outdoor seating areas. Trees require a regular pruning and repotting regimen, so the more slowly the tree grows, the less often you will have to repot it.

Fine Gardening editors

Designs for the Seasons

❮ A CENTERPIECE FOR ALL SEASONS

To keep a pot going through all seasons, plant an evergreen in the middle. Then put seasonal annuals around the outside, changing them for each season. Just be careful not to disturb the evergreen's roots when planting the annuals. To protect the roots, you could plant the evergreen in its own pot and then bury that pot in the soil of the larger container.

Fine Gardening editors

SHRUBS ADD WINTER COLOR

Shrubs such as 'Red Sprite' winterberry (*Ilex verticillata* 'Red Sprite'), redtwig dogwoods (*Cornus alba* and cvs.), and red osier dogwoods fill out a container nicely. They take a back seat to more colorful specimens during the summer, but in winter, they light up dreary days with colorful berries or stems.

June Hutson, Missouri

DEPENDABLE WINTER FOLIAGE

Persistent foliage, even in winter, makes Japanese sweet flag a great plant for containers where there is ample moisture. It can even be grown in pots without drainage holes, opening up more possibilities for its use. 'Ogon' seems to be the most evergreen in the family and finds its way into many of my arrangements.

Rita Randolph, Jackson, Tennessee

RELY ON STRONG FORMS THAT STAND OUT IN THE SNOW

Many people feel that winter containers are a waste of time because they can't be appreciated when covered in snow or ice. Using strong architectural forms in your containers will allow them to stand out even when encased in snow. Hardy 'Green Mountain' boxwood has this kind of profile. Its clean, simple lines stand out against almost any backdrop, especially when dusted with snow.

Muffin Evander, Maryland

KEEP IT GREEN ALL YEAR

Lime green is a daydreamy, whimsical color that can't be resisted. Even in winter, 'Citronelle' heuchera maintains its striking chartreuse color. Its dense foliage fills out even more during brief breaks in frigid weather. As a thick filler, 'Citronelle' gives containers visual appeal all year long.

Rita Randolph, Jackson, Tennessee

THE KEYS TO SUCCESSFUL WINTER CONTAINERS

The general rule for container-plant survival through the winter is to use plants hardy to at least two zones colder than your USDA hardiness zone; this, however, is not always a steadfast rule. Many trees, shrubs, and perennials that are hardy in your zone will live and even thrive in containers through all four seasons. In this case, a frost-proof pot with a drainage hole is important. Fiberglass, lead, iron, heavy plastic, and stone are the best weather-resistant containers to use; terra-cotta will eventually expand and crack with repeated freezing and thawing.

Muffin Evander, Maryland

COLOR ME HAPPY

'Angelina' sedum tops the list of my favorite hardy succulents because its summer cloak of chartreuse foliage turns a luscious, brilliant, coppery orange in winter. Its juicy leaves cascade out of pots and baskets, and it makes a welcome companion plant at a time when choices may be few and far between.

Rita Randolph, Jackson, Tennessee

1 'Quartz Creek' corkscrew rush   2 Cyclamen   3 Compact Innocence® nemesia   4 Variegated English ivy

FRAGRANT FLOWERS SWEETEN A POT IN SPRING

You can never go wrong with fragrance. A pot of cyclamen and nemesia always draws my friends and visitors over to take a sniff. These plants appreciate the cool spring weather. Adding evergreen corkscrew rush creates a linear form with year-round appeal—just change its partners. In the summer months, corkscrew rush mixes well with low-growing annuals of all kinds, like dwarf lantana and alternanthera.

Rita Randolph, Jackson, Tennessee

1 'Super Sugar Snap' pea   2 'Tangerine Gem' marigold   3 'Fernleaf' dill   4 Matrix Deep Blue Blotch pansy   5 'Red Sails' lettuce
6 'Buttercrunch' lettuce   7 Curly parsley

AN EARLY SPRING MEDLEY

I love growing peas in containers because they provide a unique vertical accent. You'll need a trellis for support for the peas. Then add edible spring flowers, herbs, and greens to create a delicious spring treat for both the eye and the palate. Leafy lettuce can go at the base of the teepee, while mini marigolds and purple pansies add floral accents. The fluffy dwarf 'Fernleaf' dill stands out among the broad leaves. This container would reach its peak in mid-spring; yank out the contents and replant it with some late-season vegetables.

Danielle Sherry, Niantic, Connecticut

1 'Sweet Caroline Bewitched Purple' sweet potato vine   2 'Cha Cha' cuphea   3 Senorita Rosalita® Cleome
4 'Northern Lights Lavender' Pentas   5 'Amazon Sunset' lotus vine   6 Babylon® Light Blue verbena   7 'Brilliantissima' iresine

HIGHLIGHT SOFT SUMMER PETALS WITH DARK MATES

Summer flowers attract hummingbirds and butterflies, so I often create containers that feature flowering nectar plants along with ones grown purely for their foliage. I use dark-colored leaves to dramatically outline my best bloomers, because flowering plants often don't have the most interesting foliage. I also alternate small leaves and bold leaves to add distinction among foliage plants.

Rita Randolph, Jackson, Tennessee

NEVER-ENDING COLOR

Whether used in sun or shade, crotons maintain constant color all summer. Their citrus-colored variegation is unmatched, and they can fly solo in a container or bring life to nearly any combo.

Rita Randolph, Jackson, Tennessee

BEAT THE SUMMER HEAT WITH TROPICALS

Large-leaved tropical plants really can take the heat, and they do wonders for pool decks or large patios. They can also act as an umbrella for or a backdrop to a seating area. Pairing them with blooming companions adds color and much-needed pollen and nectar, which attract wildlife.

Rita Randolph, Jackson, Tennessee

PROTECT YOUR LETTUCE FROM SUMMER HEAT

Summer plantings of lettuce are subject to heat and the burning sun, which may cause early bolting. Although young plants are less likely to bolt than older plants during the long, hot days of summer, shading further reduces this possibility. I plant summer transplants in the shade of other plants, such as tomatoes.

Lee Reich, New Paltz, New York

TROPICALS WON'T FADE IN SUMMER SUN

In our Zone 7B–8A East Coast/Mid-Atlantic area, the summers are hot and humid. The night temperatures do not drop, so many annuals are not good performers for us. The bright sun also bleaches out colors. This makes tropicals, with their bright colors and heat tolerance, ideal plants for bold containers. Our biggest challenge is fitting our favorite tropicals into our small greenhouse during the cold months.

Bill Pinkham, Carrollton, Virginia

PRETTY PEPPERS PERK UP FALL POTS

Ornamental peppers start producing fruit early in the season but come into their prime late in the season. They are indispensable for fall containers, adding both color and form.

Rita Randolph, Jackson, Tennessee

SWITCH PLANTS FOR YEAR-ROUND INTEREST

Don't just focus containers on spring and summer—make them work for you in every season. Once Jack Frost makes his fall debut, replace summer favorites with cold-tolerant kale (*Brassica oleracea* cvs., annual), pansies (*Viola* x *wittrockiana* cvs.), mums (*Chrysanthemum* spp. and cvs.), asters (*Aster* spp. and cvs.), and sedums (*Sedum* spp. and cvs.). Also try colorful stems and interesting fruits and vegetables; spray vegetables like gourds with repellents to deter squirrels. Include a full array of conifer boughs, colorful branches, cones, and berries for winter containers. In cold climates, the natural refrigeration of winter preserves the freshness of the containers until spring.

Scott Endres, Minneapolis, Minnesota

1 Bush germander   2 Supertunia® vista silverberry petunia   3 Cabana® trailing blue bacopa
4 Molimba® Mini Double White Marguerite daisy   5 'Silvery Sunproof' liriope

RECYCLE FALL FOLIAGE

Don't trash all your plants during fall cleanup. Foliage that can hang on throughout
the year should be overwintered so that you can recycle it in spring. You can jazz up a
foliage planting with cold-hardy flowering annuals, like petunia and Marguerite daisy,
which easily tuck in between persistent perennials.

Rita Randolph, Jackson, Tennessee

NO ONE WANTS TO SEE A LONELY MUM

Chrysanthemums need friends—those companion plants that meld a combo together. By adding a splash of lemongrass, you'll spice up even the most mundane mum. Grasses of all sizes are a natural fit with mums, their fine foliage adding height to the mix.

Rita Randolph, Jackson, Tennessee

Choosing Plants

SHOP FOR PLANTS IN YOUR OWN YARD

There is nothing like colorful annuals to add color and pizzazz to my summer pots. For filler plants, however, I like to shop in my own yard. Divisions of perennials—like liriope (*Lirope muscari* and cvs.), sedums (*Sedum* spp. and cvs.), hostas (*Hosta* spp. and cvs.), ornamental grasses, bleeding hearts (*Dicentra*), Artemisia (*Artemisia* spp. and cvs.), and even irises (*Iris* spp. and cvs.)—work wonderfully for adding bulk and height. An added bonus of using perennials is that the plants can be planted back in the garden in fall.

Joan Schoettelkotte, Edgewood, Kentucky

DON'T BUY IT IF YOU CAN'T SMELL IT

When you grow oregano, start with nursery-grown plants. Because the flavor can vary from plant to plant, it's a good idea to sniff and taste a leaf before you buy.

Rolfe Hagen, Alsea, Oregon

WAIT AND SEE

If you buy a plant because you love it but you don't know what to do with it, put it in a pot for a year until you can figure it out. It will add to your garden and give you time to fit it into your landscape plans for next year.

Fine Gardening editors

EASY MAINTENANCE

If you can't give your containers daily attention, choose plants that thrive on less water and require less fuss.

Deborah Silver, Sylvan Lake, Michigan

READY-TO-GO CONTAINERS GET YOU STARTED

An easy and time-saving way to fill a pot is to find a mixed container or hanging basket at a local nursery that has plants you really like in it. Transfer it to a larger container of your own and then add to the mix any other plants you find appealing.

Rita Randolph, Jackson, Tennessee

Edibles

PUNCH UP THE COLOR AND FLAVOR

Mix and match ornamentals with edibles for a striking composition. Because you harvest only a small amount of lettuce and other greens at a time, the plants stay compact and the overall composition will last.

Fine Gardening editors

PROVENCE IN A POT

Narrow your choices down to several Mediterranean herbs that have the same cultural needs. And for the sake of harmony, choose herbs with flavors that blend well. A mix of rosemary, marjoram, thyme, bay, sage, and oregano is a good choice. These plants all enjoy bright sun and well-drained soil, they grow well in containers, and they're very useful in cooking.

Mimi Luebbermann, Petaluma, California

A NO-PINCH BASIL

Affectionately called "basketball basil," 'Aristotle' is an ultra-compact Greek variety. It has a neat, rounded habit that requires no pruning to maintain its shape. The form may be unique, but 'Aristotle' nonetheless maintains a pungent, classic flavor. The plants grow to be 12 in. to 14 in. tall and wide, making them perfect for container pots or small vegetable gardens.

Danielle Sherry, Niantic, Connecticut

LEMON THYME IS AT ITS BEST IN TIGHT SPACES

Lemon thyme, known for its intense lemon aroma, can be a scraggly mat in the ground; confined in a container, however, it's an attractive, upright mound of small, pointed, glossy green leaves. As the branches grow, they spread out and trail over the container's edge; by early summer, they produce dense heads of lilac-colored flowers that last for more than a month. When the flowers are done blooming, cut back the stems and fertilize.

Jo Ann Gardner, Westport, New York

PINEAPPLE MINT IS A SWEET SENSATION

Pineapple mint has no discernible pineapple flavor but is a beautiful, spreading foliage plant with ruffled, cream-splashed green leaves that taste sweet and fruity. In the garden, it takes over damp corners, but in a container, it produces just enough leaves to fill out a medium-size pot. Pineapple mint is best grown from plants, not seeds, but it can be easily propagated using cuttings.

Jo Ann Gardner, Westport, New York

THERE'S MORE TO MARIGOLDS THAN COLOR

Marigolds don't just add color to an edible planting. The flowers from these annual plants have a lemony flavor that goes well with poultry and fish dishes.

Fine Gardening editors

HERBS IN THE SHADE

In full shade, only a handful of herbs will do well. Use mints, violets, sweet woodruff, and cervil for an attractive planting. Experiment a little until you know exactly how far you can push it; you may be pleasantly surprised.

Frédérique Lavoipierre, Sebastopol, California

TARRAGON HAS A SHORT POT LIFE

Tarragon grows well in a container, but only for a season. After that, its roots outgrow the pot and it loses flavor. You'll need to repot it into a larger pot or transplant it into the garden.

Andrew Yeoman, Vancouver Island, British Columbia, Canada

THE MANY FACES OF ROSEMARY

Whatever look you want, there's a rosemary for you. Shrub varieties of rosemary come in dwarf, medium, and tall sizes, with compact, open, or spiraling habits of growth. Prostrate forms grow outward and will trail over the sides of a pot.

Theresa Mieseler, Chaska, Minnesota

1 'Lesbos' Greek columnar basil   2 'Pesto Perpetuo' basil   3 'Black Pearl' ornamental pepper
4 'Bull's Blood' beet   5 'Calypso Red' ornamental pepper

GREENS LOOK GOOD AND TASTE GREAT

Many leafy greens and vegetables have beautiful foliage color, last all summer, and pack a flavorful punch. Use only the safest potting mixes and fertilizers for these plants so that no toxins show up in your salad bowl.

Rita Randolph, Jackson, Tennessee

TONS OF TOMATOES

Determinate tomatoes are usually better for containers because they don't get huge and unwieldy. 'Sweet-n-Neat Cherry Red' (*Lycopersicon esculentum* 'Sweet-n-Neat Cherry Red') is the perfect tomato for containers because the plant reaches only 14 in. tall. This dwarf determinate tomato produces lots of sweet-tasting small fruit, but it will need some staking to support its heavy fruit load.

Fine Gardening editors

THE RIGHT TOMATO

For tomatoes, I recommend 'Rutgers', with medium-size fruit, or the cherry variety 'Tiny Tim'. Both do well in containers. Stay away from the big-fruited varieties, which demand lots of root space.

Joan Bankemper, New York, New York

TRIED-AND-TRUE SAUCE TOMATO

When space is at a premium but you want a multipurpose paste tomato, plant 'Saucy'. Its determinate, disease-resistant vines are compact but prolific. The easy-to-peel fruit grows in clusters that hold well on the vine until you're ready to pick them.

Kris Wetherbee, western Oregon

CRAMPED QUARTERS?
NOT A PROBLEM

Not all edibles will thrive in tight spaces. When choosing vegetables for your pots, try to find bush varieties that won't take up a lot of space but will give you good yields. You could also try a dwarf variety of the vegetable you want. You can find dwarf cucumbers, dwarf bush beans, and many others.

Fine Gardening editors

CERTAIN PICKLERS PROVIDE THE
BEST CRUNCH

Cucumber vines are attractive enough that a pot of them wouldn't look out of place on the patio. There are dwarf varieties—including 'Bush Pickle Hybrid,' with vines only 18 in. long—suitable for growing in small spaces or even in containers. 'H-19 Little Leaf' is a particularly good candidate, with its ivylike foliage and clouds of yellow flowers.

Cass Peterson, southern Pennsylvania

CABBAGE FLAVOR

Ornamental cabbage, although usually grown for its beauty, is edible. It is slightly milder than regular cabbage but does not hold its brilliant color once cooked.

Fine Gardening editors

SQUASH SPILLERS

Yes, you can even grow squash in a container. You can train dwarf varieties to grow up a trellis. But the plant can also act as the spiller in your container, trailing over the edge and adding interest to the pot.

Fine Gardening editors

Drought-Tolerant Plants

1 **Blue agave**   2 **Silver bush**   3 **'Ogdon' sedum**   4 **Dwarf agave**

COMBOS THAT WORK

I often add groundcover succulents and drought-tolerant plants to the base of larger succulents for extra interest and diversity. Blue agave makes a great star plant on its own, but it is enhanced by supporting plants with striking color or texture to make a great combination.

Scott Endres, Minneapolis, Minnesota

WATER-WISE PLANTS LIKE IT TIGHT

The best container choices for water-wise, or drought-adapted, plants are pots that closely match the size of the plant's root mass and have ample drainage holes. Minimizing the size of the container keeps the soil mass smaller, which helps it dry out more quickly. Most of these plants come from habitats where soil is as scarce as rain, so they are quite happy in tight quarters. It will be obvious when it's time to upgrade certain specimens to larger pots: The plant will outgrow its container, becoming top-heavy and out of scale with the pot, yet still be robust and healthy.

Tom Peace, Colorado and Texas

PLANTS THAT THRIVE ON NEGLECT

One of the most popular and easy-to-find groups of drought-adapted plants is succulents, which store water in their leaves. This broad group includes the cold-hardy hens and chicks (*Sempervivum* spp. and cvs.) and sedums (*Sedums* spp. and cvs.) as well as the more tender graptopetalums (*Graptopetalum* spp.) and echeverias (*Echeveria* spp. and cvs.).

Another easy-to-find group is the large, diverse cactus family, which eschews leaves for succulent stems that hold moisture through dry times. They come in various prickly forms, including barrels, pads, mounds, and clumps. All cacti grow well in containers—just be careful of their spines and of the tiny but more obnoxious glochids, the small clusters of stiff hairs that can get stuck in your skin.

Tom Peace, Colorado and Texas

IT GOES WITH EVERYTHING >

Zebra plant makes an excellent accent in succulent gardens. It's interesting up close, but it won't steal the show from its more dramatic neighbors.

Scott Endres, Minneapolis, Minnesota

< SUCCULENTS AS SCULPTURE

More than being just accent plants, succulents form the sculptural backbone of arid gardens. Plants such as agaves (*Agave* spp. and cvs.) come in varieties that thrive in every corner of the region. Combine their star-shaped form with spherical barrel-type cacti for excellent sculptural effects.

Scott Calhoun, Tucson, Arizona

1 African milk tree   2 Peacock echeveria   3 Dwarf jade   4 'Midnight' aloe   5 Paddle plant

SUCCULENTS ARE A MUST-HAVE

If there is one hot plant group I couldn't live without, it would be succulents. Their luxurious textures, shapes, and colors offer incomparable bold structure. I often create succulent gardens as miniature landscapes, which are perfect for outdoor dining tables or centerpieces for seating areas, where you can appreciate them at close proximity.

Scott Endres, Minneapolis, Minnesota

Water Gardens

◀ ADD PLANTS WITH CARE

Pay close attention to everything that goes into your water features. Many people often add plants directly to their outdoor water gardens and ponds, but this isn't a good idea. String algae will form with pretty much every plant you introduce into the water—and once you get it, you can't get rid of it. Instead, I designed a pot to get some attractive green foliage into my koi pond without attracting string algae. The pot also keeps the koi from nibbling on the plants and hides some unsightly pipes.

Inta Krombolz, West Chester, Pennsylvania

WATER-CONTAINER BASICS

While any container that holds water can become a water container, choose one with a suitable depth for the plants you will be growing. Use the size of your largest plants as a guide, and make sure that the container can provide the right depth. Smaller plants can be set on stones or bricks to raise them.

If your perfect container has a hole in the bottom, put tape across the bottom of the hole, then plug the hole from the inside with plumber's putty. A container made from a porous material like terra-cotta will need to have a sealant applied before it will hold water.

Greg Speichert, northwest Indiana

ADD HEIGHT TO YOUR WATER GARDEN

If you want a little variety in your water garden, use bricks or upside-down containers to stagger the height of plants.

Fine Gardening editors

HOW TO PLANT
A WATER CONTAINER

Place plants in the container, keeping them in their original pots. If the pots do not have a top layer of pea gravel, add one to prevent soil leakage, which would dirty the water. Be sure to set plants at the proper depth as you arrange them.

Greg Speichert, northwest Indiana

A TROUGH FOR
A WATER GARDEN

Any metal container can work as a water garden. Just be sure to locate the pot in a shady spot, since metal heats up in the sun and can cook the roots of the plants.

Jeff Day, eastern Pennsylvania

KEEPING WATER GARDENS CLEAN

If you're worried about the stuff on the top of the water, like mosquitoes or algae, overflow the container every few days and it will float away. This is especially important to do if you don't have a bubbler.

Fine Gardening editors

A PLANT THAT HELPS
A WATER GARDEN

Papyrus is a great plant for water containers. It looks good and aerates water enough that mosquitoes don't like it (so the water doesn't have to be moving).

Fine Gardening editors

'CRUSHED ICE' ARROWHEAD MAKES A SPLASH

The bold foliage and clean white flowers of arrowheads (*Sagittaria* spp. and cvs.) make them great plants for water containers. Easy to grow in sun to light shade, they are rampant runners and can fill a container.

Arrowheads vary widely in height and leaf shape. I like 'Crushed Ice' arrowhead (*Sagittaria graminea* 'Crushed Ice') for a container because it is a great bloomer and grows to only 1 ft. tall and 1 ft. wide. Best of all are the slender variegated leaves that are in proportion to a container but still provide visual interest. Where the summers get hot, 'Crushed Ice' will benefit from afternoon shade.

Greg Speichert, northwest Indiana

DWARF PARROT FEATHER CARPETS THE WATER SURFACE

Dwarf parrot feather (*Myriophyllum papillosum* var. *pulcherrima*) is a more refined relative of the common species and is perfect for water containers because it gets only half as tall (4 in.) as its ubiquitous cousin.

Dwarf parrot feather needs only a small, 4-in.-diameter pot in which to grow, but it will spread over the surface of the water, hiding the pots of other plants and spilling over the edge of the container. Because it will float, dwarf parrot feather can be grown in deep water. Just don't submerge it.

Greg Speichert, northwest Indiana

POTS & PLANTERS

Pick a Pot   102
Not Your Typical Containers   110
Window Boxes   118
Hanging Baskets   128
Care   136

Pick a Pot

AN INFORMAL LOOK

Unglazed containers offer the ideal start-ing point for woodland-inspired designs because they often come in earth tones, whereas other rustic designs can incorpo-rate pastels or bold color schemes, colored ceramic containers, or simple wooden barrels.

Karen Chapman, Seattle, Washington

CONCRETE CONTAINERS CAN BE SIMPLE YET STYLISH

If you're looking for a straightforward, contemporary container, consider concrete. You can soften the sharp edges of the planter with your plants or add sculptural elements to break up the modern lines.

Scott Endres, Minneapolis, Minnesota

DRY-CAST LIMESTONE MAKES A MODERN "ANTIQUE"

Less expensive than solid limestone, dry-cast limestone vessels mimic pots that have been around since Roman times. The natural color ranges from warm white to soft tan, but the material can be tinted or the natural color can be altered with an applied wash. Suitable for all seasons, dry-cast limestone is frost-proof and withstands the ravages of weather year-round.

Fine Gardening editors

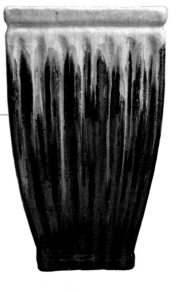

GLAZED TERRA-COTTA IS ALL ABOUT COLOR

With such a wide variety of colors available, glazed pots can be integrated into nearly any setting and are purchased primarily for their bold good looks. These pots are actually just typical terra-cotta covered in a glaze. But glazed terra-cotta tends to hold up better to weathering than regular terra-cotta because the clay is baked at higher temperatures, resulting in stronger, less permeable pots better suited to handling changes in weather. When glaze is baked onto the outer surface, it seals the exterior of the pot, making it even more resilient. The terra-cotta is still exposed on the inside of the pot, so some winter protection is required.

Fine Gardening editors

SEALING TERRA-COTTA

If you're attached to the idea of terra-cotta but really need a material that isn't so porous, use a masonry sealer on the terra-cotta to make it less porous.

Fine Gardening editors

BEYOND TERRA-COTTA

When choosing a container, you'll need to balance aesthetics with practicality. The traditional terra-cotta pot looks wonderful, but it requires faithful watering, because the planting medium dries out quicker in porous clay than it does in glazed ceramic or plastic. If you are a lax waterer, or if your best sunny location is in a hot spot, choose a glazed or plastic pot. If you're wedded to the terra-cotta look, buy a plastic pot one size smaller than your terra-cotta container and slip it inside. Conceal any visible plastic rim with sphagnum moss.

Mimi Luebbermann, Petaluma, California

FABULOUS FIBERGLASS

Fiberglass is more expensive than plastic but is worth it. Feather-light and durable, it is also flexible enough to give when the soil freezes and therefore can be left outdoors in the winter. Fiberglass can be molded into any shape and made to look like many materials, from stone to wood to metal.

Fine Gardening editors

WINTERPROOF CONTAINERS

One of the most backbreaking jobs in the garden is lugging countless containers up the basement stairs in spring and back down in fall. All right, so maybe your husband handles most of the work, but if he didn't help, he'd have to listen to you worry all winter that your pots might crack from the freeze-and-thaw cycle of winter. So to save your husband's time for other items on the honey-do list, try adding to your collection some pots made out of concrete and good-quality fiberglass (see the photo at left), both of which boast all-season sturdiness. Keeping containers on the patio also provides a place to add winter interest with some ever-green boughs and berries.

Michelle Gervais, New Milford, Connecticut

POTS THAT CAN TAKE THE HEAT

New plastic and fiberglass containers in light colors deflect heat, so they make a good choice if you live in a hot climate.

Fine Gardening editors

A CONSISTENT LOOK

Use pots that look alike, such as all terra-cotta or all concrete, to maintain a consistent style. Polystyrene containers that mimic natural materials are fine alongside the real thing. It's the look of the container that counts, not what it's made of.

Steve Silk, Farmington, Connecticut

MODERN MATERIALS

Composite and polyresin are lightweight synthetic newcomers that replicate the look and texture of hand-carved stone, weathered and mossy concrete, and also the patina of old plaster, copper, or bronze. These pots are frost-resistant and durable, and they provide some insulation at only a fraction of the cost of the real thing.

Fine Gardening editors

BIGGER IS BETTER

Use large containers for more soil capacity and root volume. I especially like wide, low-profile bowls. Large containers make more of a statement than small ones, but don't be afraid to mix sizes and groupings to create impact.

Bill Pinkham, Carrollton, Virginia

Not Your Typical Containers

MIX IT UP

Reclaimed containers add style and sometimes a sense of humor to your arrangements.
Think beyond pots to baskets and even attractive kitchen items such as old teapots.
And don't be afraid to group a diverse mix together—just make sure not to overdo it.

Jeff Day, eastern Pennsylvania

A BARREL OF BEAUTY

Barrels make lovely mini gardens, provided all the plants in them have similar sun and moisture requirements. Be playful about mixing vegetables, fruits, herbs, and flowers.

Sylvia Thompson, California

A RECIPE FOR A HYPERTUFA MIX

Recipes for small quantities of concrete are usually specified by proportion—so many units of cement to so many units of gravel, and so on. A good hypertufa mix is 2 parts Portland cement, 3 parts peat moss, 3 parts perlite, and a handful of fibermesh.

Jeff Day, eastern Pennsylvania

A BOTTOMLESS BASKET

When the bottom of a nicely aged apple basket fell out because of water damage, I was going to throw it out. Then it occurred to me that it might make a nice "container" for a clump of speedwell (*Veronica spicata* cv.) growing in one of my beds. I slipped it over the plant in the spring and anchored the bottom to the ground with a few garden staples. The weathered basket looks great with the lavender-blue blooms, and it also helps support the plant's vertical spires.

Susan Colliton, La Crosse, Wisconsin

DECORATE YOUR HYPERTUFA PLANTER

If you're making your own hypertufa container, then you've got a lot more decorative options than you would if you simply bought a premade container. You can add shells, stones, mosaics, or other decorative materials to your planter. Just push the pieces in place once you've put the hypertufa mix onto the mold.

Jeff Day, eastern Pennsylvania

AN HERB IN EVERY POCKET

Strawberry jars aren't just for strawberries. For a space-saving herb garden, put one herb in each pocket of a strawberry jar. Try salvia, oregano, winter savory, golden lemon thyme, silver thyme, rosemary, Vietnamese coriander, tricolor sage, and French tarragon (see the photo at left). Or you can use less variety and grow just a couple of types.

Jeff Day, eastern Pennsylvania

LETTUCE CENTERPIECE

Instead of sowing your lettuce seeds in a flat, try sowing them directly into a low-sided dish or bowl. The lettuce will keep germinating after you cut some, so you'll have a continuous supply. Keep the dish on your tabletop for an attractive—and productive—centerpiece.

Fine Gardening editors

TIERS MADE EASY

You can use benches and wooden tiers to get a tiered look for your plants, but if you don't have the appropriate furniture, try this instead: Sink a pot partway into the soil of a larger pot, and then plant around it. You will get the same tiered effect.

Fine Gardening editors

CHIMNEY-FLUE LINERS CREATE A GARDEN

Chimney-flue liners or old terra-cotta drain tiles turned on end can be set directly on the ground or partially buried, and because they have no bottoms, drainage isn't a problem. By playing around with their placement, you can add architectural interest and charm to your garden.

Flue liners are available from building or masonry suppliers. They are 1 ft. square and 2 ft. long, but they can be shortened using a circular saw with a masonry blade. Like most terra-cotta, the flue liners can spall—that is, they flake off in pieces with repeated exposure to rain, snow, and freezing. Our liners usually last five to eight years before their antique charm seems excessive.

Ron Zimmerman, Fall City, Washington

EASY EMBELLISHMENTS

When it comes to painting pots, the design possibilities are endless. Try a freehand design, or start with a stencil until you're comfortable experimenting on your own. Just keep in mind that temperatures that are too hot or too cold change drying times and may leave you with a sticky mess or prevent crackling if you're using crackle paint. The ideal temperature is 60°F to 80°F.

Jeff Day, eastern Pennsylvania

Window Boxes

SIZE MATTERS

Match your window box to your window. The window box should be about as long as your window, measured from side to side, including the wood trim. If you can't get a plastic liner the same size as the window box, get one a little smaller, but build the planter to match the window's measurements. Wedge the liner in place with some wood scraps or stones.

Jeff Day, eastern Pennsylvania

1 'Wojo's Jem' vinca vine   2 Bonfire® begonia   3 Bauer's dracaena

ADD FOCUS WHERE THERE IS NONE

A window box can draw focus and create interest in a part of the backyard living area where inground plantings are not an option.

Scott Endres, Minneapolis, Minnesota

SECOND-STORY BOXES

If you put a window box on a second-story window, make sure there is ready access for watering, such as from a screen that is easy to pop up. Otherwise you'll be on a ladder often for watering.

Fine Gardening editors

THE RIGHT SPOT IN A WINDOW BOX

Try to place thirstier plants toward the back and middle of the boxes, where the soil stays moist the longest.

Frédérique Lavoipierre, Sebastopol, California

NOT YOUR TYPICAL WINDOW-BOX FLOWERS

Succulents are a good choice for window boxes because you don't have to water them very often. They also have a nice texture that looks good when viewed up close from the inside of the window.

Fine Gardening editors

WINDOW BOXES NEED MORE THAN RAIN

Remember, if you have wide eaves, no rainfall will reach your boxes, and regular watering will be necessary. A small drip system on a timer works well.

Frédérique Lavoipierre, Sebastopol, California

1 'Freckles' coleus   2 Fusion Glow impatiens   3 Catalina® Blue wishbone flower   4 Sweet Caroline® Light Green sweet potato vine

PAIRED BOXES NEED VARIETY

If your house has a pair of windows on either side of the front door, repetition is crucial for a cohesive design. But making each box an exact duplicate of the other can be boring. To add more visual interest, consider planting each box to be a mirror image of the other.

Gary R. Keim, Lansdowne, Pennsylvania

WINTER CHEER

Window boxes don't have to be confined to looking pretty just in the summer. Add evergreens and holly for the winter season to make the box look festive from indoors and out.

Jeff Day, eastern Pennsylvania

QUICK CHANGES

When planting your window boxes, use a tray with plantings in separate containers
so that you can lift them out. This makes it easy to replace plants if they die but also
makes adding seasonal décor to the boxes a snap.

Fine Gardening editors

MAKE A SHADY BOX SHINE

You might think you can't have a window box on a window that receives no direct sunlight, but you can. Instead of focusing on color, think about contrasting leaf shapes and textures in shady boxes. In this photo, an Australian fern anchors the planting with its height and mass. The foliage of 'Lifelime' coleus contrasts with the shape and texture of the fern but complements its color. The coleus should be trimmed periodically to make them bushy and to keep them from overwhelming the fern. A variegated ivy dangles from beneath the fern and coleus, softening and hiding the box.

Gary Keim, Lansdowne, Pennsylvania

1 'Polly' African mask   2 Dragon Wing® Pink begonia   3 Caladium   4 Golden creeping Jenny
5 Summer Wave® Amethyst wishbone flower

LOOK BEYOND THE USUAL SUSPECTS

Flower boxes need to pack a punch if they are going to grab attention from the street. Forgo many of the plants normally used in boxes for something more eye-catching. In the box above, the African mask and the begonia immediately grab your interest.

Gary Keim, Lansdowne, Pennsylvania

KEEP AIR FLOWING

Choose sturdy, well-built boxes that are as wide and deep as possible for your window. Be sure to install boxes securely, as they'll be heavy when full, even with a lightweight potting mix. We install boxes to leave a gap between the back of the box and the siding to allow for air circulation, which is especially important if your house has wood siding.

Frédérique Lavoipierre, Sebastopol, California

HANG IT RIGHT

For strength, the hooks holding your window box should go into the studs. Find the studs from inside the house with an electronic stud finder. Measure where the studs are in relation to the center of the window, then measure again from outside and mark the stud location on the siding.

In brick walls, you'll need to drill a hole and install a fastener called an anchor to hold the hook in place. Drill the holes with a masonry bit. The size of the holes will depend on the size of the anchor you use. When you buy the anchors, ask what size hole they require, and buy a matching bit.

Jeff Day, eastern Pennsylvania

BOXES NEED HOLES >

Put holes in the bottom of a window box for drainage or else water will just sit in the box and rot the plants.

Fine Gardening editors

DEEP ROOTS WON'T WORK IN BOXES

When choosing plants for a window box, be sure to select plants with shallow root systems. Plants whose roots need a lot of room, like tomatoes, would get too cramped in the confines of a window box.

Fine Gardening editors

Hanging Baskets

❮ NO-CARE FLOWERS FOR BASKETS

Plants in hanging baskets are harder to get to, so you need to choose carefully. Avoid plants that need deadheading, like traditional petunias. You really want self-cleaning flowers so that you don't need to worry about any care other than watering.

Fine Gardening editors

BASKETS AREN'T JUST FOR FLOWERS

Experiment with planting fruits and vegetables in a hanging basket in the air instead of in a pot on the ground. Try cherry tomatoes, Malabar spinach, and strawberries for starters.

Sylvia Thompson, California

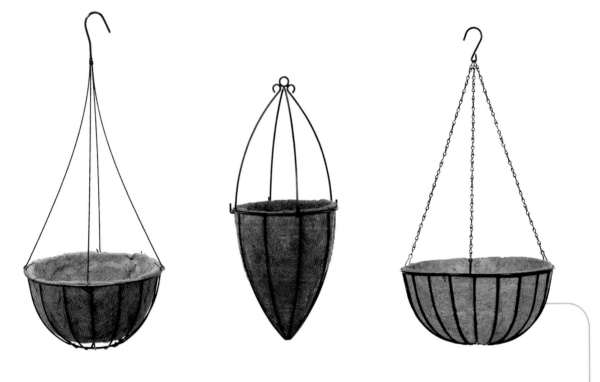

CHOOSE A BASKET

When it comes to baskets, size—or, in this case, volume—does matter. The volume of the basket is directly related to the amount of water your hanging garden can retain; if you select a basket that is too small, you'll have to water daily, if not more often. A larger basket can make taller columns or posts look more in scale with your house or landscape. I use baskets that have open sides so that I can cut slits in the liner in a checkerboard pattern for planting.

C. Dwayne Jones, Waynesboro, Virginia

NOT TOO SHORT, NOT TOO LONG

Is the chain too long? Most hanging baskets come with a set of three chains and a hook for hanging. If the chains are too long, shorten them by removing links with needlenose pliers. Remove as many links as you want until the chain is just the right length.

Jeff Day, eastern Pennsylvania

BIGGER IS BETTER

The pot your hanging plant comes in is usually too small for the planting, which means you'll have to water it all the time to keep it healthy. Instead, buy a container that's meant to be hung, or pick a favorite pot, put a fabric hanger around it, and transplant the plant into that.

Fine Gardening editors

DON'T FORGET THE DRIPS

When you position your hanging baskets, don't forget to consider where people will sit. After you water the baskets, water will drain from them, and you don't want your baskets dripping on someone's head.

Fine Gardening editors

KEEP DANGER OUT OF REACH

If you want a plant that could be poisonous but you have children who touch everything, try putting the plant in a hanging basket to keep it out of reach.

Fine Gardening editors

TOMATOES IN A BASKET

Hanging baskets aren't just for flowers. 'Tumbling Tom' is a good variety of tomato for a hanging basket. You'll be able to reach up and grab a tomato anytime. Just be sure to place the basket where a tomato won't drop on unsuspecting guests or make a mess splattering on a patio.

Fine Gardening editors

SPRUCE UP YOUR BASKET

Anything is more attractive than the container you get when you buy a hanging basket. Transfer the plants to another pot or basket; if you can't find something that will work, paint the basket from the nursery.

Fine Gardening editors

A FULL BASKET >

You don't have to plant only the top of a hanging basket. For a fuller look, plant the sides too. Use a wire basket so you can cut through the open sides and the permeable liner, then plant through the liner for a full basket.

C. Dwayne Jones, Waynesboro, Virginia

STAGGER YOUR PLANTS

To ensure maximum coverage while preserving visibility in your hanging basket, place plants in a checkerboard pattern. After spacing plants evenly in the first row, create the next row so that its plants fall between, not directly behind, those in front.

C. Dwayne Jones, Waynesboro, Virginia

A HANGING BASKET'S BEST LINER

Supamoss is a product made of dyed, recycled cotton fibers that are sewn to thin green plastic sheeting. The tiny needle holes allow for water to drain, yet the plastic membrane conserves the majority of the water for the plants. It is easy to poke holes into this material for planting, and the green mossy look is appealing.

C. Dwayne Jones, Waynesboro, Virginia

INSERT A WATER RESERVOIR IN YOUR BASKET

To help with aeration and watering, I insert into my baskets a vertical 8-in. to 10-in. section of black slotted drainpipe, available at any hardware store. I adjust the length so that 2 in. to 3 in. are exposed above the final soil level; this ensures that the drainpipe does not fill with potting soil during rainfall or waterings. I place the pipe so that the end sits 4 in. to 5 in. above the bottom of the basket. If the drainpipe hits the bottom of the basket, water will simply drain right out of the basket instead of filling the surrounding area. The pipe directs the water toward the bottom of the basket, which is the first place to dry out.

C. Dwayne Jones, Waynesboro, Virginia

BASKETS ARE THIRSTY

Hanging baskets can dry out quickly and need frequent watering. Don't use water-absorbing crystals in them because the crystals will absorb all the water instead of keeping it available for your thirsty plants.

Fine Gardening editors

HOLD MOISTURE BETTER

To help hold moisture for a longer period of time, place plastic with slits cut into it on top of the fiber lining in your basket, then add the plants.

Fine Gardening editors

Care

❮ EXTEND THE LIFE OF WOOD PLANTERS

Even though there are parts of the planter that won't show, paint everything anyway. Paint does more than simply make something look good. It also protects the wood from the weather. Your planter will last much longer if you take the time to paint the entire thing.

If you want to avoid priming and painting, apply pigmented exterior stain, often called deck stain. It comes in a variety of colors. Brush it on and you're done. For a darker color and better protection, apply a second coat.

Jeff Day, eastern Pennsylvania

HEAT CAN HURT, TOO

Scorching temperatures can kill roots just as easily as frigid ones can. If you live in an area where the mercury regularly tops 100°F, you should know how to keep your containers cool. One way to do this is to group them together. This not only raises the relative humidity in the immediate area but also keeps the sun's rays from baking the pots toward the back of the bunch. You can also put one container inside another. The resulting double thickness will help insulate the soil.

Fine Gardening editors

OVERWINTERING POTS

If the soil in your pots gets wet and freezes, it will expand and crack the pots. So unless your containers are frost-proof, you'll need to bring them indoors for the winter in cold climates. But go ahead and leave the soil in place— it just needs to be dry, not necessarily warm— making a garden shed perfect for storing the pots.

Fine Gardening editors

STACKING POTS

Add newspaper in between pots when storing them so that they don't stick together when you stack them. This helps prevent cracking not only while they're stored but also when you try separating them in the spring.

Fine Gardening editors

INSULATE POTS FOR OUTDOOR WINTER STORAGE

If you can't bring your pots out of the weather in cold-winter climates, it's best to wrap the pots with bubble wrap during the winter to waterproof as well as insulate them. You can leave the soil in the pot, but both the soil and the pot must be completely dry before you wrap them. Cover the pot's top and sides with a couple of layers of bubble wrap. Secure the wrap by circling the pot, top and bottom, with clear weather-stripping tape, which you can buy at a hardware store.

Jeff Day, eastern Pennsylvania

GLAZED CERAMIC IS FRAGILE

Treat glazed containers kindly by storing them indoors in the winter.

Fine Gardening editors

POT FEET PROTECT YOUR POTS

Freezing temperatures make it absolutely necessary to lift containers off the ground to keep the base from freezing and breaking. Pot feet do the lifting and ensure that potentially freezing water will drain off quickly and not collect in or under the container.

Pot feet also protect your pots from the blazing sun on a patio. When you put pots directly on a stone patio in a spot that gets full sun, the pots will heat up—and so will the plant roots. The plants will definitely need more water, but it's even better to put the pots up on feet so that they don't directly touch the patio.

Rita Randolph, Jackson, Tennessee

PROTECT WINTER CONTAINERS

When using high-fired stoneware that will remain outdoors in winter, consider using one with a vase-shaped sidewall so that moist, freezing soil will have room to expand, both upward and outward. Lining the sides of your container with bubble wrap provides extra room for expansion and helps hold in moisture (see the photo above).

If your container is urn-shaped and tapers in at the top, however, it will not be able to handle any expansion from freezing. You'll need to find a properly fitted liner, such as a nursery bucket or other plastic pot, to drop into it (see the right photo above). I pick a liner that allows for an inch or two of space between it and the pot walls. The liner also allows you to easily remove the entire plant combo when necessary.

Rita Randolph, Jackson, Tennessee

CLEAN POTS TO DETER DISEASE

A good maintenance routine starts with well-prepared containers. To help prevent disease, thoroughly scrub all previously used pots with dish soap and hot water. Then sterilize them with a mixture of 2 parts white vinegar to 1 part water, with a handful of kosher rock salt added. You can also use a 10% bleach solution. To sterilize small pots, run them through the dishwasher after cleaning off the debris, then plant in them while they're still damp.

Andrea Albert, Boynton Beach, Florida

TAKING CARE OF IRON

Although iron is prone to rusting, yearly applications of a weather-resistant sealant can help slow down the aging process.

Fine Gardening editors

PLANTING
&
MAINTENANCE

Soil	144
Potting	156
Watering	169
Pruning	179
Pests & Other Problems	187
Overwintering	190

Soil

SANDY TOPDRESSING HOLDS IN MOISTURE

If your fully grown pots dry out so fast that watering them becomes a major chore, try mulching with some handfuls of a sand, bark, and granular fertilizer mix. When this combo is spread evenly on top and watered, the sand sifts down into the root area and helps hold in extra moisture.

Rita Randolph, Jackson, Tennessee

A MIX FOR ANNUALS

I create a mix high in nutrients for my annuals so that they'll pump out flowers. Because the worm castings and chicken manure provide enough nutrients to last throughout the season and the pine bark continues to increase fertility as it decomposes, this mix requires little feeding on my part:

- 1 part expanded slate
- 1 part composted chicken manure
- 1 part worm castings
- 1 part composted pine bark
- 1 part coarse river sand

Bobbie Saul, Atlanta, Georgia

START WITH YOUR OWN SOIL

When removing a plant from the nursery container, also remove the soil from the plant's roots. Put good soil in your container, then add the plant. You can get more in your pot this way, and the soil is better.

Fine Gardening editors

THE RIGHT PORTIONS ARE KEY

Don't overfertilize, because the salts build up in a container. One plant might absorb a lot of the fertilizer and overcrowd some of the smaller plants, which would require you to cut it back, increasing your maintenance.

Fine Gardening editors

COMPOSTED CHICKEN MANURE

Composted chicken manure has the highest natural-nutrient content available. Use it to amp up the fertility of your mix, but never use it raw: It must be composted or it will burn plant roots. Buy it by the bag at a garden center or feed store.

ROCK DUST

Rock dust helps you mimic native soils. This powder made of pulverized stone contains trace nutrients and mineral from bedrock, the natural source material of all soils. Get it free at a local quarry, or buy a 5-pound bag from mail-order sources.

CHARCOAL PELLETS

Charcoal pellets decrease the odor of decomposition. The organic matter used in some mix recipes is often so rich that it can result in a smelly pot. Adding charcoal pellets, available at aquarium stores, absorbs the odor while improving drainage.

PLAYGROUND SAND

Playground sand ensures a loose mix. The same bag of sand used in kids' sandboxes can improve the drainage in your containers, helping your plants thrive. Available at any hardware or home-improvement store, a 50-pound bag typically costs less than $5.

Daryl Beyers

ADD GRAVEL TO SOIL MIXES FOR EXCELLENT WINTER DRAINAGE

Add a little gravel to the potting media when planting conifers. They appreciate rich soils and regular watering but require excellent drainage. Choose an inert gravel in a color that complements your container and plant choices. A large stone is a nice architectural touch. Topdressing with stones and gravel or a piece of driftwood also helps retain your potting soil during winter weather.

Rita Randolph, Jackson, Tennessee

WATER PLANTS NEED THEIR OWN FOOD

I use a fertilizer intended for water plants because conditions underwater are different from those underground. I feed my plants monthly until the water reaches about 80°F, and then I fertilize every two weeks.

Greg Speichert, northwest Indiana

SOIL FOR WATER CONTAINERS

When it comes to choosing the best potting medium for aquatic plants, there is no one right answer. Ideally, the medium should supply anchorage, fertilization, and moisture retention. The potting mix should also suit the needs of the gardener. It should be easy to use and odorless and not make the pond look muddy. Affordability and availability are also important factors. A few of the best options are:

- Clay soil
- Kitty litter
- Sand
- Cocoa fiber
- Pebbles and pea gravel

Greg Speichert, northwest Indiana

WEATHER DETERMINES SOIL MIX FOR WATER-WISE PLANTS

For areas with dry summers, use a soilless mix that doesn't contain much peat moss, and add perlite or pumice gravel to it. If you live in a region with moist, humid summers, use a soilless mix, and add coarse grit or pea gravel to it because extra drainage is a must. You can also create your own mix of 50% pea gravel and 50% compost/pine bark. Be aware, however, that this mix will add a lot of weight to your containers. Don't add moisture-retaining polymer crystals to either of these potting mixes, because water misers like it dry.

Tom Peace, Colorado and Texas

CUSTOMIZE YOUR MIX TO SUIT YOUR PLANTS

Whether you use a manufactured or homemade potting mix, it's a good idea to have extra mineral aggregate and organic material on hand to suit some plants' special needs:

- Add extra aggregate for plants that like their soil on the dry side.
- Add extra peat moss to mixes for plants that prefer consistently moist soils.
- Grow top-heavy plants in a mix amended with calcined clay or sand to add weight to the pot.

Lee Reich, New Paltz, New York

FERTILIZE FLOWERS FOR SUCCESS

Incorporate slow-release fertilizer into the soil before planting. But it is still critical to continue to apply liquid fertilizer every week to 10 days. Nutrients are quickly leached out of the soil with the regular watering that is necessary to grow a great container of plants.

Nancy and Pierre Moitrier, Maryland

FERTILIZE ONCE FOR LOW-MAINTENANCE PLANTS

Even low-maintenance plants potted in complete soil mixes with starter fertilizer will need additional fertilizer later in the season. I recommend applying a second round of quick-response fertilizer as a topdressing in July. "Quick response" means that half of the nutrients are available right away, giving the plants an initial boost, and the rest are slowly released.

Scott Endres, Minneapolis, Minnesota

Iron and trace elements   **Soy meal**   **Greensand**   **Kelp meal**

ADD THE PROPER MIX TO EVERY TOMATO POT

A rich fertilizer mix spurs the growth of tomatoes in pots. The recipe includes iron and trace elements, soy meal, greensand, and kelp meal. Nutrients should be well-mixed with soil before the tomato containers are filled.

Sandra B. Rubino, Pensacola, Florida

KNOW YOUR PLANTS' FEEDING REQUIREMENTS

Nutrients leach quickly out of containers, so before planting edibles in containers be sure to find out what their requirements are. For cherry tomatoes, for instance, a good fertilizer should have more phosphorus than nitrogen. Peppers will probably need a fair amount of nitrogen when they're first growing but more phosphorus once they start producing fruit.

Fine Gardening editors

"DOCTOR UP" YOUR VEGETABLE MIX

You'll need to amend your potting soil with compost and other nutrients, because edibles are heavy feeders. A standard potting mix doesn't contain enough nutrients to sustain a container full of vegetables all season long, and dousing your pots with liquid synthetic fertilizers isn't ideal because you're going to eat the contents. Here's a quick-fix recipe that will ensure success when combined with an occasional dose of liquid organic fertilizer:

- 3 parts traditional potting soil
- 1 part compost
- 1 part peat moss
- A spadeful of leaf mulch

Danielle Sherry, Niantic, Connecticut

TAKING CARE OF THYME

Making more thyme is easy. Because this herb has roots all along its stem, you can simply cut off a piece (any length), stick it in some potting soil, and keep it well watered. In no time, you will have a new plant.

Fine Gardening editors

LESS FERTILIZER IS MORE FOR BASIL

Because basil is a leaf crop, you might be tempted to fertilize heavily. If you do, you may indeed get large plants, but it will be at the expense of flavor. If you feel you must feed them, use a liquid fertilizer that will provide for quick, early growth but then will be gone by the time the plants are ready to harvest.

Shep Ogden, Burlington, Vermont

NO-FUSS PARSLEY

Like its brethren in the garden, potted parsley likes rich, moist soil. I use half garden soil and half starting mix, and I fertilize with liquid emulsion. Potted parsley also seems to appreciate a little afternoon shade.

Ashley Miller, Trumansburg, New York

ROSY GROWING CONDITIONS FOR ROSEMARY

To grow rosemary in pots, select potting soil with a minimum of peat moss, which is acid, as rosemary likes an alkaline pH. Add enough sand for superb drainage. The surface should dry out between waterings, but the soil should never be completely dry.

Sylvia Thompson, California

THE RIGHT POTTING MIX FOR HERBS

Potted herbs do well in compost and a sterile medium of peat moss, vermiculite, and perlite, with quick- and slow-release fertilizer (compost is slow release). For all pots, throw enough compost into each pot to allow room for adding a depth of 6 in. more sterile medium. Sparingly mix in water-absorbing polymers; they lessen the need for watering by making the best use of available moisture. There are two exceptions to this recipe: For nasturtiums, omit the compost and add extra vermiculite. For thyme, add grit (fine gravel or coarse sand).

Jo Ann Gardner, Westport, New York

SAVE MONEY BY BUYING BIG

You can save time and money by purchasing the items you need for your potting mix in bulk and making large batches to set aside for a later date or to share with your gardening friends.

Daryl Beyers

Potting

START 'ALASKA' NASTURTIUM FROM SEED

In late spring, when temperatures rise, sow seeds outdoors directly in containers in two batches about a week apart. Two sowings will ensure a longer season of bloom. Don't fertilize, and add a couple handfuls of perlite to the growing medium to reduce nutrients so that plants produce more flowers than leaves.

Jo Ann Gardner, Westport, New York

DEALING WITH A POT-BOUND PLANT

Roots are tougher than you might think, so don't be afraid to get rough with them. Until you convince girdled roots that they have room to spread out and grow, they will continue thinking that they're in the pot and continue to strangle the plant. Break up the roots by whatever means necessary. This might mean gently teasing them loose, ripping them apart with your hands, or slicing into the root mass with a shovel.

Fine Gardening editors

NEATER PLANTING

Start planting in the center of the container, and add plants from the center out. That way you can place them appropriately without getting all the plants covered with soil.

Fine Gardening editors

OPPOSITES CAN LIVE TOGETHER

Don't believe the old adage that plants with different growing conditions can't coexist in the same pot. If you want to use plants that require two different conditions—like wet soil and dry soil—keep one in a separate container within the larger container and treat its soil needs separately.

Scott Endres, Minneapolis, Minnesota

False bottom

Plastic pot as insert

FILL THE VOID IN LARGE POTS TO SAVE ON SOIL

Oversize or extra-heavy containers can be soil hogs, but you can save on potting mix and give your back a reprieve by finding the perfect-size, lightweight plastic pot to fit into your jumbo pot (see the right photo above). If you're potting up a container where the sidewalls taper uniformly, you can often save on soil volume and spare the extra plastic pot by lifting up the floor of your decorative container with a false bottom made expressly for this purpose (see the left photo above); one such planter insert is Ups-A-Daisy® (www. ups-a-daisy.com). This product still allows proper drainage for your plants, can be kept year after year, and is available at most garden centers. It doesn't fit straight-sided pots, however, so you might need to fill the void in those containers with plastic jugs.

Rita Randolph, Jackson, Tennessee

SAUCERS SERVE AS FALSE CONTAINER BOTTOMS

Instead of filling a large container full of potting soil, or working with messy bags of packing peanuts, or buying false bottoms, I make my own. I select a saucer one or two times smaller than the opening of the pot I'm working with and drop it into the pot, wedging it in tightly. Then I drill holes in the saucer for drainage. My large pots are much lighter now, and I don't have to use as much soil to fill them.

Donna Muellner, St. Louis, Missouri

CONTAINER PLANTS NEED HARDENING OFF, TOO

Homegrown seedlings are perfect for your containers. But be sure to follow the guidelines for hardening off plants before you plant them in containers and put them outside. Gradually expose them to sun and wind before giving them a permanent home in containers.

Fine Gardening editors

CHECK SOIL LEVELS

About two weeks after planting your pots, add more soil on the top; typically the soil gets watered down.

Fine Gardening editors

GRAVEL MEANS GREAT DRAINAGE FOR SUCCULENTS

If you're growing succulents, add gravel to the potting soil for even better drainage. Then top-dress the container with a little more gravel, using blue-gray or warm, earth-toned stones. This not only is attractive but also keeps water and soil from splashing onto the plants. This final benefit is especially important if you are growing succulents. The last thing you want to have to do is use more water to wash dirt off their leaves.

Rita Randolph, Jackson, Tennessee

IGNORE DRAINAGE MYTHS

Drainage is impeded by a coarse layer of material buried in the soil. Whether planting trees or shrubs in soil with poor drainage or potting perennials in a container, the recommendation has been to put a layer of gravel in the bottom of the planting hole or container to facilitate water movement. These efforts actually impede drainage because a layer of water forms just above the coarse layer. This perched water table forms whenever there is a dramatic change in soil porosity.

So ignore this recommendation for improving drainage. Do not layer coarse materials into the bottom of planting holes. For the bottom of flowerpots, use only what is needed to keep the soil from washing through the hole, such as a bit of screening.

Lee Reich, New Paltz, New York

LINING TERRA-COTTA POTS SAVES WATER

Terra-cotta containers can certainly be a challenge to keep watered during the hot summer months, but lining the inside of a pot with a plastic bag can cut down on evaporation from the sidewalls. Be sure to provide drainage by cutting plenty of holes in the bottom of the bag.

Rita Randolph, Jackson, Tennessee

LAYERING BULBS

To plant a container with different species of bulbs, plant the larger bulbs first, then cover them with soil and plant the smaller bulbs. Fill the container with soil to just below the rim.

Richard Hartlage

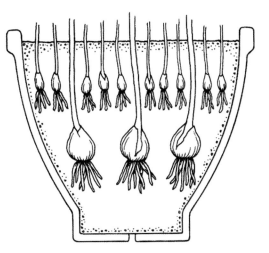

CAGE TOMATOES FOR THEIR OWN GOOD

Concrete reinforcing wire provides sturdy support for tomato vines and a perfect frame for attaching anti-bug netting.

Sandra B. Rubino, Pensacola, Florida

BIGGER IS BETTER FOR GARLIC

Break apart a large head of garlic and plant only the biggest cloves. The bigger the clove, the greater the likelihood it will yield a nice big head of garlic. Save the smaller cloves for the kitchen.

Ruth Lively, New Haven, Connecticut

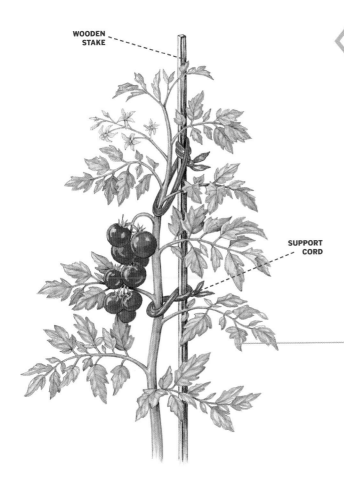

WOODEN STAKE

SUPPORT CORD

SUCCESSFUL TOMATO STAKING

Be sure to encourage tall, strong tomato plants by staking them right from the get-go. Get a sturdy stake 3 ft. to 4 ft. tall. Wood or metal works best. If you use a wimpy stake, your plants could topple over. Drive the stake deep into the ground a few inches from the plant base to make sure it doesn't work its way out in strong winds or heavy rains. Tie a soft cord or cloth from the stake to the plant stem. Don't tie the cord directly under any branches with flower buds (the weight of new fruits may cause the stem to snap).

Fine Gardening editors

EVEN LANKY CHERRY TOMATOES HAVE A CHANCE

If you buy nursery-grown plants, find the stockiest ones you can, without flowers or fruit. If only lanky plants are available, don't despair. Bury them sideways several inches deeper than they were in the pots so that more of the stem is in the soil. The plants will reach skyward, and more roots will develop along the buried stems.

Alice Krinsky Formiga, Litchfield, Connecticut

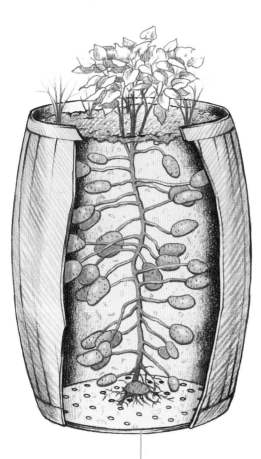

HIGH YIELD POTATO PLANTING TECHNIQUE

You can grow 100 lb. of potatoes or more in a container with this neat trick. Take a large container—a whole wooden barrel or cask is ideal. Less attractive but equally functional is a 55-gallon oil drum without a top. Make sure it is thoroughly clean inside. Punch or drill lots of ½-in. holes in the bottom for drainage.

Shovel about 8 in. of sandy soil into the bottom. Plant five seed potatoes and water them in. Wait until the plants are 6 in. to 8 in. tall. Shovel in more soil, loosely and gently, until just one or two leaves of each plant remain above soil level. Moisten the soil. Wait until the plants have grown another 6 in. to 8 in. Cover them almost completely again.

Repeat this procedure until the barrel is full. To keep Colorado potato beetles away, staple floating row cover over the top. Make sure you keep the soil in the barrel evenly moist but not wet. What you will end up with are five potato plants with roots several feet deep.

When the tops have flowered and died back, tip the barrel on its side. Be careful, as it will be heavy. The barrel will be filled with potatoes.

Peter Garnham, Amagansett, New York

POTATOES IN A CAN

For several years I resigned myself to the idea that this tuberous plant was not suitable for a container garden. But where there's a will, there's a way. With a little research and experimentation, I decided that all I needed was the right container. And I found that in the most unlikely of places: the kitchen garbage can.

Potatoes need a soil depth of about 2 ft. to grow in, so select a clean can that will accommodate that amount of soil. A plastic can is best because it is weatherproof and you can easily drill drainage holes in it. Potatoes will rot if left to sit in wet soil, so drill several drainage holes in the base of the container as well as along the sides—1 in. to 2 in. above the bottom—to ensure plenty of drainage. Once you create the drainage holes, place your can in a sunny location and fill it to 5 in. from the top with potting mix.

Press your potato starts about 6 in. into the soil with the eyes facing toward the sun. Plant only one or two starts per can; otherwise, the soil will quickly be sapped of nutrients. Cover the starts with soil. Because the potato tubers will grow in the soil that lies between the surface and the original potato start, it's important to mound additional soil on top of the emerging plant. Remember to leave some green foliage above the soil line so that the leaves can photosynthesize. You may have to mound soil on the plant a couple of times in the early stages of growth.

Brandi Spade, Middletown, Connecticut

Mound soil mix to form a dome.

Spread the apricot tree's root around the dome, making sure the tree is centered in the pot.

POTTING A MINIATURE APRICOT TREE

In a separate container, mix potting soil, compost, wood ash, and sand, then fill the planting pot halfway full. I mound the soil in the center of the pot to create a small dome and then set the tree in the pot, splaying the roots around the mound. Be sure the tree is centered in the pot, then add soil to cover the roots. Don't bury the knob on the trunk where the tree was grafted. The soil height should be no more than an inch above the point where the roots first splay from the trunk. Wet the soil thoroughly, until water drains from the pot's hole, and firm the soil around the roots.

Laura McGrath, Watertown, Massachusetts

Watering

WATERING WANDS MAKE WATERING EASIER

For plants in pots, and especially those in hanging baskets, a watering wand is the ultimate device for anyone who hasn't rigged up a drip-irrigation system. The wand gives a few extra feet of reach, so it's great for targeting plants in hanging baskets, pots on the ground, or container plantings positioned behind other containers or set into a border. It also makes it easy to get underneath the foliage so you know the water actually gets to the soil.

Fine Gardening editors

USE SAUCERS TO SAVE WATER FOR LATER

I often place saucers under containers that are located in hot, sunny locations to help the soil retain moisture longer. The saucers also help when the soil is so dry that water just runs off the surface. By having water sit in the saucer, the overly dry soil has a chance to wick up the moisture. I avoid placing saucers under pots that are located in shady sites, as they can keep the pots too damp, thus killing the plants. For the same reason, I also remove the saucers during particularly rainy spells.

Jennifer Benner, Roxbury, Connecticut

WATERING PARCHED CONTAINERS

When container plantings get too dry, the soil shrinks away from the sides of the planter; then, when you water, the water runs down the inside of the pot instead of soaking into the soil where the plant's root can take it in. One way to fix this problem is to poke small holes in the soil around the plant with a pencil then slowly pour water directly into the holes. The water will soak into the soil, and the roots will get what they need.

Lisa Greene, Perham, Minnesota

PROVIDE A STEADY SUPPLY OF WATER

My strategy is to water containers thoroughly when the soil surface becomes dry to the touch. During the hottest part of the summer, this can mean watering at least every day. I add water to each pot until I see it draining from the bottom, which ensures that moisture has reached the deepest roots. I also avoid watering at the end of the day. Without sunlight and warmth on leaves, the foliage stays wet longer, making it more susceptible to foliar diseases.

Jennifer Benner, Roxbury, Connecticut

OVERWATERING

It's amazing how many plants are killed by too much water. You should always make sure your container has sufficient drainage holes in the bottom. If the pot is bigger than your head, it should have more than one hole. I've seen pots the size of a small car with one pinkie-size hole in the middle. That isn't going to drain. Buy a cordless drill and a masonry bit, and go to town. Place your pot flat on a concrete or stone surface, then drill a hole on the back side so that the water can run out. Otherwise, the next time it rains, your plant will "steam" in the heat or rot in the cold.

Jimmy Turner, Dallas, Texas

MIX IN SOME MAGIC CRYSTALS

Moisture-retaining soil additives can minimize the need to water. In years with excessive rain or with pots located in shade, however, the soil tends to stay too moist.

Jennifer Benner, Roxbury, Connecticut

MOISTURE RINGS

I grow a lot of herbs on my kitchen windowsill. When I'm going to be away for a week or so, I cut rings from several layers of newspaper, moisten them, and place them on the soil around the plants. I've found that doing this helps limit moisture loss.

Mandy Stowe, Beatrice, Nebraska

WATER LESS WITH WATER CRYSTALS

I sometimes use water-absorbing crystals in my container plantings. They can make the difference between watering daily and watering weekly, though I'd never trust them to keep the thirstiest of plants happy for much more than an extra day or two without a real drenching. I do have a few containers placed outside the range of easy hose coverage, and I don't get to them quite as often as I should. For them, the crystals make all the difference between a radiant display and what I might charitably call a dried arrangement.

Wet the crystals before you mix them into the soil. Once wet, the crystals expand to many times their original size thanks to all the water they've absorbed. The first time I used water-retaining crystals, I mixed them dry with soil, planted up a pot, and then added water. The crystals expanded so much that there was nowhere for them to go but out of the pot in great oozings of gelatin-like slime. Used properly and with restraint, prewetted water-retaining crystals can help create a far prettier garden picture.

Steve Silk, Farmington, Connecticut

TWO-STEP WATERING

Water your containers in two stages. The first time you water, do it slowly. Make the rounds of all your containers, then come back and water some more. This ensures that the water soaks in.

Fine Gardening editors

TRICKLE-DOWN CONTAINER WATERING

I group my container gardens on my second-story deck so that the drip watering system also waters the plants and pots on the patio beneath. By strategically positioning the pots above and below, the irrigation system can do double duty. This system saves money, time, and many gallons of water.

Robert Dunlop Miclean, Pasadena, Maryland

KEEPING WET IN NEW ENGLAND

In the Northeast, most containers in full sun need to be watered at least once a day.

Leslie Schaler, Amherst, Massachusetts

KEEPING MINT HEALTHY

Water mint deeply and heavily once in a while rather than watering it lightly more often. To help prevent the spread of leaf diseases such as rust, water the soil and not the foliage.

Ron Zimmerman, Fall City, Washington

DRIP IRRIGATION

One drip-irrigation kit for container plants may be all you need if you have municipal water and your container plants have similar water requirements. If your plants have diverse water requirements, you'll need a wider range of emitters than a single kit provides. You can mix components from different manufacturers.

Steve Silk, Farmington, Connecticut

MAKE YOUR CONTAINERS SELF-WATERING

Watering is one activity that you can't eliminate, but you can make it easier. Use watering systems with anchored emitters on a patio packed full of containers. Set them up on a timer and you'll barely have to think about watering. The only thing you need to do is pay attention to the weather so that you can adjust your watering schedule accordingly. Even the right system requires some care, but it sure beats frantically lugging watering cans around to water your plants before you leave for work in the morning.

Michelle Gervais, New Milford, Connecticut

WATER-WISE PLANTS LIKE IT DRY

Even though these plants like it dry, they need to be watered periodically. It is critical, however, to give them a dry spell between waterings. That dry time can last for days or even weeks with no harm done to the plants. When you do water them, it's important to be thorough, repeating the process a couple of times to guarantee that the entire soil mass gets wet.

Tom Peace, Denver and Texas

CHIVES THRIVE WITHOUT LOTS OF WATER

Chives don't thrive on neglect, but it's certainly easy to keep them content. Chives like average soil, very good drainage, and four to six hours of sun daily. They don't require a lot of water—only two or three times a week.

Susan Belsinger, Brookville, Maryland

Pruning

CONSISTENT CARE FOR LUSH POTS

Containers need more than just water. Containers that are given consistent care will thrive with abundant growth and more flowers. A three-part maintenance routine of fertilizer, primping, and pruning is essential to getting great-looking containers.

Fine Gardening editors

PRUNE PLANTS BACK INTO SHAPE

Some plants need a total overhaul by midsummer. If a plant is appearing less productive and attractive overall, I cut all the stems back by as much as half to a leaf node or growing point. The plant is usually up and running again in a couple of weeks. If the idea of cutting the whole plant back intimidates you, do it gradually over three weeks by cutting one-third of the stems back each week. Avoid pruning your plants during the heat of the day, which is stressful for the plants. Prune them, instead, in the morning or evening, when the stems are firm yet bendable.

Jennifer Benner, Roxbury, Connecticut

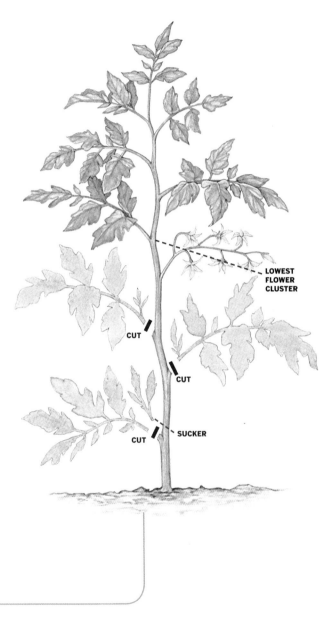

LOWEST
FLOWER
CLUSTER

CUT

CUT

CUT — SUCKER

EARLY PRUNING ENCOURAGES STRONG TOMATO STEMS >

Be sure to remove all suckers and leaves below the first flower cluster on your tomato plants. Aside from making the plant stronger, pruning gets it off the ground (helping to ward off diseases) and gives it more room to grow. Never prune tomatoes when the leaves are wet.

Ruth Lively, New Haven, Connecticut

UNTHINNED CARROTS

THINNED CARROTS

AVOID THE ALIEN EFFECT WITH ROOT VEGGIES

Unthinned root vegetables become deformed as they develop underground—
if they develop at all. These unsightly veggies are still perfectly edible, but they
are not as large and harder to peel, cut, and use in the kitchen. Thinned plants
produce better, overall.

Cass Peterson, southern Pennsylvania

MAXIMIZE HERB FLAVOR

Herbs taste best if harvested just at the
point when they begin to flower, before
the essential oils in the leaves are re-
directed to the production of seed. To hold
back flowering as long as possible, simply
snip off all developing flower buds as soon
as you see them. In basil, they are easy to
recognize by their stacked, nearly leafless
structure (see the photo at left).

Shep Ogden, Burlington, Vermont

Slice about 2 in. of soil from the bottom and the outside.

ONCE-A-YEAR PRUNING FOR ROSEMARY

Large pots of rosemary should be transplanted twice a year. When the plant finally gets too big to move to a larger pot, remove it from the pot and shave off about 2 in. of roots and soil from both the outside edge and bottom. When doing this sort of invasive pruning, make sure to cut part of the top of the plant back to compensate for the root pruning. You can then put the plant back into the same pot and replenish with new soil. Transplanting will stimulate new growth.

Theresa Mieseler, Chaska, Minnesota

DIVIDE TO CONQUER MINT >

When the center of a mint plant no longer sends out sprigs, divide the root ball into thirds and replant in new soil.

Ron Zimmerman, Fall City, Washington

A DRASTIC HAIRCUT ENCOURAGES NEW HERB GROWTH

Herbs can be fully harvested about once a month during the growing season. This regular pruning encourages new growth and maximizes leaf yield. To fully harvest annual herbs, such as basil, cut all the stems back to just above the bottom two sets of leaves. Perennial herbs, like sage, should be cut back to about one-third of their height, also just above a set of leaves. As you collect your harvest, keep the newly cut stems out of the sun or they will quickly wilt.

Susan Belsinger, Brookville, Maryland

EDIT OCCASIONALLY

Constructive editing allows slow-growing cultivars time to catch up while encouraging strong, sustainable growth on plants that get pruned back. Pinch fast-growing characters as needed throughout the season to maintain equal distribution of interest among the players. For coleus, pinch at planting to encourage strong, bushy plants and also as needed for the duration of the season.

Scott Endres, Minneapolis, Minnesota

FULLER MINT WITH JUST A PINCH

For bushier, healthier mint, pinch off the top two sets of leaves regularly.

Ron Zimmerman, Fall City, Washington

DEADHEAD FOR MORE BLOOMS

Deadheading means you cut off spent blooms to prevent a plant from going to seed too quickly. This will, in most cases, force the plant into a second round of lush blooms.

Fine Gardening editors

Pests &
Other Problems

❮ SAFETY FIRST ⎯⎯⎯⎯⎯⎯⎯

When you're considering your options for
protecting your edibles from pests, use soap
sprays. They are the safest for spraying on food.

Fine Gardening editors

SLUG-FREE CONTAINERS

Although a band of copper around the container will keep slugs from eating your herbs, I discovered they can still crawl through the hole in the bottom of your pot. A copper scouring pad placed over the hole before the potting soil is added works well to keep slugs out. The pad allows water to drain, but the sharp edges of the copper filaments deter slugs from inching their way inside the pot.

Jo Anne Durdock, New Milford, Connecticut

KEEP PESTS AT BAY

To deter many insects and diseases, place unpeeled garlic cloves an inch deep in the soil near the rim of each pot—about three cloves in a 14-in.-diameter pot. They sprout thin leaves that resemble crocus foliage.

Andrea Albert, Boynton Beach, Florida

NO-SLUG LETTUCE

Slugs love lettuce, but luckily they seem to prefer beer. A few saucers of stale beer help them drown their sorrow and themselves. Sugar water also works, but unfortunately, bees like it even more than slugs.

Peter Garnham, East Hampton, New York

SQUIRREL-PROOFING

Squirrels can be a problem in the spring, digging up freshly planted flowers. To protect the flowers and roots, place big rocks on the soil surface right after planting up until the time the flowers fill in.

Fine Gardening editors

ATTRACT GOOD BUGS TO YOUR TOMATOES

I plant herbs such as cilantro and dill near my tomatoes and let them go to flower. They attract beneficial insects that keep pests, such as hornworms, under control.

Alice Krinsky Formiga, Litchfield, Connecticut

AN EASY FIX

If a plant gets a disease or pest, take the plant out, buy a different plant, and replant in the same place. Powdery mildew, for instance, will affect a certain plant, so it won't transfer to the soil and affect other plants.

Fine Gardening editors

GET TO KNOW THE GOOD BUGS

To create a welcoming habitat for your insect helpers, first you need to know something about them. A good way to start is to grab a hand lens and a picture book of insects and take a rough census of your resident population. If you've avoided using pesticides and have a variety of plants growing, you may find many allies already present.

Joe Queirolo, San Ramon, California

Overwintering

‹ LIGHT IS THE KEY FOR ROSEMARY SUCCESS

Most rosemary grown in pots will survive light freezes, but you should bring the pots indoors before the temperature drops below 30°F. Successfully growing rosemary indoors requires good sunlight—the more the better—and ideally a southern exposure. If the plant is large, rotate it weekly so all sides of the plant receive sunlight. Wiry growth often indicates inadequate light. If you can't increase natural light, consider using artificial light. Rosemary grows best indoors at cool temperatures (55°F to 60°F).

Theresa Mieseler, Chaska, Minnesota

SOME KITCHEN HERBS CAN BEAR THE COLD

Evergreen rosemary and parsley are two essential herbs in my recipes, and with just a little protection from the elements, they will grow wonderfully through the winter. They both thrive in a relatively small pot that I pull indoors only during the worst weather.

Rita Randolph, Jackson, Tennessee

MORE MINT NEXT YEAR

When winter approaches, cut mints right to the ground. This will make them more prolific the following year. In cold climates, protect the roots by piling mulch around the pots or by bringing the pots into the garage until spring. The same severe pruning works on leggy plants in any season. They'll quickly send up new shoots.

Ron Zimmerman, Fall City, Washington

BRING LEMON VERBENA INSIDE FOR WINTER

When you grow lemon verbena in a container, it can easily be moved into a cool, bright room before the first frost. Expect the plant to drop its leaves when you bring it indoors. Once this happens, cut back on water until the soil is just barely moist. Come spring, be patient. It can easily be mid-May before your lemon verbena begins to leaf out. If you fear the plant has died, break a branch to see whether it is still green inside.

Pat Battle, Flat Rock, North Carolina

OVERWINTER A TENDER PLANT

If you couldn't resist buying too many expensive, luscious tropicals for your container gardens this year, you'll need to find a way to protect your investment and keep your treasures safe over the winter until they can return to your patio next year.

The best place is a warm, bright location. Before the first frost, bring them indoors and place them in front of a sunny window. You can cut the plants back by as much as two-thirds to make them more manageable. Rotate them occasionally so that they don't become misshapen from reaching for the sun. Plants that usually make attractive houseplants (for example, begonias and coleus) are best suited to this treatment.

Many tender plants will go dormant if you place them in a cool, dark location during the winter months. Reduce your watering and fertilizing in late summer and then give them a light pruning right before the first hard frost. Drag them inside, and store them in a basement or unheated garage (someplace that won't allow them to freeze but that stays chilly). They won't need to be watered again until you place them back outside in spring. Plants like bananas and brugmansias do well with this mode of care.

Fine Gardening editors

EASY-TO-OVERWINTER TROPICALS

If you want to bring in your tropicals as house-plants during the winter, try leaving the tropical plant in its original plastic pot when you plant your container. Just drop it into a larger container, then add potting mix and the rest of the plants around the pot. In fall, you can just lift out the tropical pot, clean it up, and bring it inside for the cold season.

Melonie Ice, Ada, Michigan

BULBS NEED A SINGLE FROST

Bulbous plants should be allowed to experience a frost before being stored for the winter. Collect and store bulbous plants by type.

Steve Silk, Farmington, Connecticut

LEMON BALM NEEDS A NEW START

By the end of the season, lemon balm will have developed woody stems and can overwinter in pots. It is a short-lived perennial, however, so start new plants in spring by dividing the original plant, discarding woody growth, and repotting in fresh soil.

Jo Ann Gardner, Westport, New York

CHIVES THAT LAST

Both the common chive and the garlic chive are hardy perennials. In warmer climates like those found in Florida and southern California, chives will grow year-round, albeit slowly. In cold climates, move the pot indoors to a cool windowsill without a lot of sun.

Susan Belsinger, Brookville, Maryland

START EARLY

When you're planting a winter container, assemble your designs early enough that the plants have time to acclimate to their new pots before the first hard freeze.

Muffin Evander, Maryland

WINTER MEANS LOW-MAINTENANCE WATERING

Winter containers usually need to be checked only monthly for water to make sure they haven't dried out; when the soil eventually becomes frozen solid, watering is no longer necessary.

Muffin Evander, Maryland

KEEPING PERENNIALS OUTSIDE

Perennials make great container plants. Before the onset of winter, be sure to remove the plants from their pots and plant them in the ground. Then simply repot them in the spring.

Jeff Day, eastern Pennsylvania

KEEP ELEPHANT EARS ALIVE

To overwinter elephant ears (*Colocasia* spp. and cvs.), wait for frost to kill the foliage, cut off the dead leaves at the soil level, then stick the pot—soil and all—in an unheated basement. Next spring, your plant should being sprouting again.

Fine Gardening editors

GETTING TREES AND SHRUBS THROUGH THE WINTER

The hardiness of a woody plant for a container is an important issue. Unless I know that I can move a container into a greenhouse or dig the shrub out of the pot for the winter, I always choose shrubs that are a zone hardier than recommended for my climate. Ideally, shrubs or trees are best moved to a spot close to a house or building, preferably on the east side so that they're sheltered from winter winds. You can pile the area around the pot with straw to provide an even cozier environment. It's also important that the pots you choose be made of materials that are resistant to winter damage, such as concrete, wood, resin, or plastic.

June Hutson, Missouri

USDA Hardiness Zone Map

The zones listed in Fine Gardening are based on several zones and should be treated as general guidelines when selecting plants for your garden. Many other factors may come into play in determining healthy plant growth. Microclimates, wind, soil type, soil moisture, humidity, snow, and winter sunshine may greatly affect the adaptability of plants. For more information and to zoom in on your area, visit the map online at www.usna.usda.gov/Hardzone/ushzmap.html.

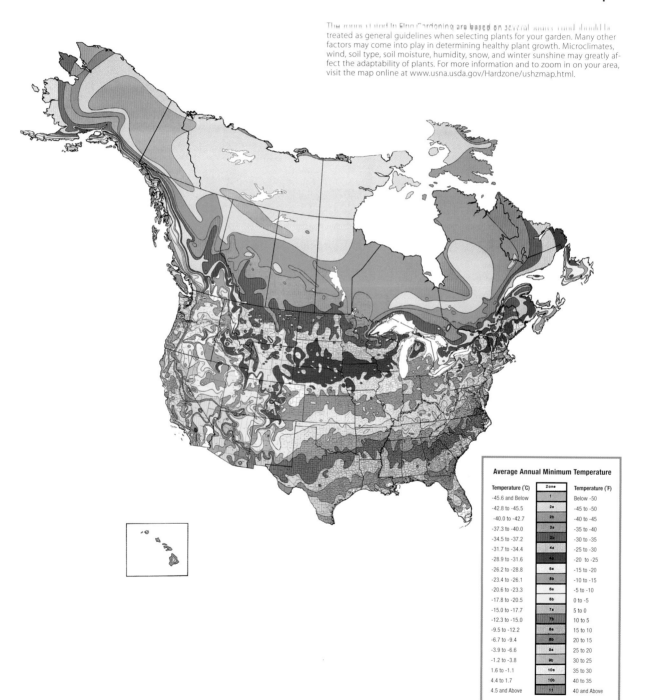

Average Annual Minimum Temperature

Temperature (°C)	Zone	Temperature (°F)
-45.6 and Below	1	Below -50
-42.8 to -45.5	2a	-45 to -50
-40.0 to -42.7	2b	-40 to -45
-37.3 to -40.0	3a	-35 to -40
-34.5 to -37.2	3b	-30 to -35
-31.7 to -34.4	4a	-25 to -30
-28.9 to -31.6	4b	-20 to -25
-26.2 to -28.8	5a	-15 to -20
-23.4 to -26.1	5b	-10 to -15
-20.6 to -23.3	6a	-5 to -10
-17.8 to -20.5	6b	0 to -5
-15.0 to -17.7	7a	5 to 0
-12.3 to -15.0	7b	10 to 5
-9.5 to -12.2	8a	15 to 10
-6.7 to -9.4	8b	20 to 15
-3.9 to -6.6	9a	25 to 20
-1.2 to -3.8	9b	30 to 25
1.6 to -1.1	10a	35 to 30
4.4 to 1.7	10b	40 to 35
4.5 and Above	11	40 and Above

Contributors

Andrea Albert grows everything from dill to datura on her patio in Boynton Beach, Florida.

Joan Bankemper is an artist whose work often has a direct garden connection.

Pat Battle oversees the garden at Highland Lake Inn in Flat Rock, North Carolina.

Susan Belsinger harvests an abundant herbal bounty each year from her garden in Brookville, Maryland.

Jennifer Benner is a horticulturist and former associate editor of *Fine Gardening*. She gardens in Roxbury, Connecticut.

Daryl Beyers is a former assistant editor of *Fine Gardening* and is a member of The Professional Gardeners' Guild.

Karen Chapman designs container gardens for herself and clients throughout the Seattle area.

Susan Colliton is a writer and fifth-generation flower gardener living in western Wisconsin. In the 1940s, her maternal grandfather planted an entire empty lot in her hometown with peonies.

Kimberly Crane is a horticulturist and owner of EarthArt in Charleston, South Carolina.

Jeff Day is a freelance editor and writer in Perkasie, Pennsylvania.

Jo-Anne Durdock gardens in New Milford, Connecticut.

Sydney Eddison is the award-winning author of numerous books on gardening and a longtime contributor to *Fine Gardening* magazine.

Scott Endres is co-owner of Tangletown Gardens, a retail garden center and landscape-design firm in Minneapolis, Minnesota.

Muffin Evander is the owner of Cultivated Designs, a container-garden design business based in Maryland.

Alice Krinsky Formiga formerly worked as the trial garden manager at Renee's Garden Seeds in Felton, California, and Shepherd's Garden Seeds in Litchfield, Connecticut. She currently works as a web content coordinator for eOrganic at http://www.extension.org/organic_production.

Deanne Fortnam is a master decorative artist and avid container gardener in Nashua, New Hampshire.

Christine Froelich is a freelance garden designer and writer. She is also the executive director of the Rochester Civic Garden Center in Rochester, New York.

Stephen Gabor, along with **Patrick Allen**, is a principal of gabor + allen, a design-build practice in Venice, California.

Jo Ann Gardner, author of *Gardens of Use and Delight*, writes and gardens from her home and farm in Westport, New York.

Peter Garnham is a Cornell master gardener and market gardener in East Hampton, New York, where he runs East End Community Organic Farm.

Michelle Gervais, an associate editor of *Fine Gardening*, tends her containers in New Milford, Connecticut.

Lisa Greene gardens in Perham, Minnesota.

Flora Grubb is co-owner of Flora Grubb Gardens in San Francisco, California.

Rolfe Hagen owns The Thyme Garden nursery in Alsea, Oregon. For more information about The Thyme Garden Herb Company, visit www.thymegarden.com.

Jennie Hammill is a passionate gardener, piano teacher, and accomplished woodworker in Seattle, Washington.

Richard Hartlage is the author of *Bold Vision for the Garden*.

June Hutson is supervisor of the Kemper Home Demonstration Gardens at the Missouri Botanical Garden.

Melonie Ice is a Michigan State University master gardener in Ada, Michigan.

C. Dwayne Jones is a horticulturist and the superintendent of parks and horticulture in Waynesboro, Virginia.

Gary R. Keim is a garden designer based in Lansdowne, Pennsylvania.

Inta Krombolz gardens deep in the woods of West Chester, Pennsylvania, and likes to create welded garden statuary in her spare time.

Frédérique Lavoipierre grows herbs and kitchen garden plants at her Shoestring Nursery in Sebastopol, California.

Ruth Lively is a former senior editor for *Kitchen Gardener*. She grows garlic by the dozens in her garden in New Haven, Connecticut.

Mimi Luebbermann, co-author of *Little Herb Gardens*, lives in Petaluma, California.

Laura McGrath designs and cares for gardens and container plantings in greater Boston. She enjoys finding ways to bring fruits and vegetables to even the smallest urban spaces.

Robert Dunlop Miclean gardens in Pasadena, Maryland.

Theresa Mieseler and her husband, Jim, specialize in growing herbs at Shady Acres Herb Farm in Chaska, Minnesota.

Ashley Miller gardens in Trumansburg, New York.

Nancy and Pierre Moitrier are the owners of Designs for Greener Gardens, a company specializing in quality horticultural care. They craft fine garden creations and container combinations in the Annapolis and Baltimore, Maryland, areas.

Donna Muellner gardens in St. Louis, Missouri.

Dee Nash has been gardening in the red dirt of Oklahoma for more than 20 years and lives outside Guthrie, Oklahoma.

Shep Ogden is the former owner of The Cook's Garden in Burlington, Vermont.

Tom Peace is a garden designer and lecturer who hangs his hat in Colorado and Texas.

Cass Peterson runs Flickerville Mountain Farm, a market garden in southern Pennsylvania.

Bill Pinkham is a retired landscape designer from Carrollton, Virginia.

Joe Queirolo manages Crow Canyon Gardens, which belongs to the City of San Ramon, California.

Rita Randolph uses plants collected from across the country to create her inspiring, seasonal container designs at Randolph's Greenhouses in Jackson, Tennessee.

Lee Reich, author of *The Pruning Book*, is a soil scientist who gardens in New Paltz, New York.

Rizaniño "Riz" Reyes, a plantsperson and landscape consultant, owns RHR Horticulture & Landwave Gardens in Shoreline, Washington.

Linda Roark owns Artistic Succulents, in Los Altos, California, and designs containers with succulents, perennials, and annuals. Linda is also a volunteer gardener at Elizabeth Gamble Garden in Palo Alto, California.

Ray Rogers is the author of 3 gardening books, including *Coleus: Rainbow Foliage for Containers and Gardens*. He lives in North Brunswick, New Jersey.

Sandra B. Rubino tends her courtyard garden in Pensacola, Florida.

Leslie Schaler is communications program coordinator at the University of Massachusetts Amherst Libraries.

Joan Schoettelkotte gardens in Edgewood, Kentucky.

Dennis Schrader is co-owner of Landcraft Environments Ltd., a wholesale greenhouse company on Long Island, New York.

Jill Schroer has been a master gardener for 20 years. She has taught classes on container gardening and vegetable gardening.

Danielle Sherry, a *Fine Gardening* associate editor, never has enough space for vegetables.

Steve Silk tends his diverse collection of container plantings in Farmington, Connecticut.

Deborah Silver is owner and operator of Deborah Silver & Co., Detroit Garden Works, and the Branch studio in Sylvan Lake, Michigan.

Greg Speichert, coauthor of *Encyclopedia of Water Garden Plants*, lives in northwest Indiana.

Mandy Stowe gardens in Beatrice, Nebraska.

Rexford Howard Talbert has been a member of the Herb Society of America for 44 years. He writes about herbs for many magazines, is a speaker on herbal subjects, and has received the Herb Society of America's Nancy Putnam Howard Award for Horticultural Excellence.

Sylvia Thompson is a former contributing editor of *Kitchen Gardener*. She is the author of *The Kitchen Garden* and *The Kitchen Garden Cookbook*.

Cookie Trivet gardens in Millfield, Ohio.

Jimmy Turner is senior director of gardens at the Dallas Arboretum and Botanical Garden in Dallas, Texas.

Kris Wetherbee is an internationally published author, writer, lifelong organic gardener, and former certified organic market grower. For more of Kris's articles on gardening and food, visit www.kriswetherbee.com.

Andrew Yeoman and Noel Richardson run Ravenhill Herb Farm, on Vancouver Island, British Columbia, Canada.

Ron Zimmerman is the owner of The Herbfarm, a farm and restaurant in Woodinville, Washington.

Credits

PHOTOS

Steve Aitken, © The Taunton Press, Inc.: p. 64, 96 (top), 98, 99, 121, 124, 125, 129, 133, 134, 143 (top), 169, 173

Jennifer Benner, © The Taunton Press, Inc.: p. vi (top center: center; bottom center: right), 46, 49 (left), 52, 56, 77, 92, 101 (bottom left), 104, 114, 139 (right)

Krista Hicks Benson, © The Taunton Press, Inc.: p. 146

Darryl Beyers, © The Taunton Press, Inc.: p. 7, 93 (bottom), 145

Katy Binder, © The Taunton Press, Inc.: p. 5 (top center: left; bottom: right), 101 (bottom right), 143 (top center: left)

John Bray, © The Taunton Press, Inc.: p. 84, 150, 164

Jennifer Brown, © The Taunton Press, Inc.: p. vi (bottom left), 16 (right), 21, 91, 110, 122, 177

© Jennifer Cheung and Steven Nisson: p. ii, 79, 152

© Donna Chiarelli: p. 101 (top), 108

Steven Cominsky, © The Taunton Press, Inc.: p. 137, 171, 182 (top)

Courtesy Kimberly Crane: p. 41

Julie Curtis: p. 105, 107

Dorling Kindersley/www.dkimages.com: 93 (top)

Courtesy Scott Endres: p. 19, 25 (left)

Stephanie Fagan, © The Taunton Press, Inc.: p. vi (top: left and right), 5 (bottom center: center and right), 36, 101 (center left), 143 (bottom center: right)

Fine Gardening staff, © The Taunton Press, Inc.: p. 141

Michelle Gervais, © The Taunton Press, Inc.: p. vi (top center: right; bottom: right), 6, 10 (right), 30, 42, 47, 48, 55, 57 (left), 59, 60, 61, 65, 68, 69, 72, 73, 74, 75, 85, 144, 147, 158 (left), 160, 162, 174, 179, 180, 194

Billy Goodnick: p. 49 (right)

Boyd Hagen, © The Taunton Press, Inc.: p. 80 (top), 86 (bottom), 143 (bottom center), 184, 185, 192

© Saxon Holt: p. 83 (bottom), 126, 151, 154, 187

Janet M. Jemmott, © The Taunton Press, Inc.: p. 66, 87, 88 (right), 112, 153, 183, 190

Bill Johnson: p. vi (bottom center: left), 67

Jefferson Kolle, © The Taunton Press, Inc.: p. 168, 182 (bottom)

© Mark Lohman: p. vi (top center: left; bottom center: center), 5 (bottom: left), 22, 25 (right), 63, 109, 111, 115, 123, 127, 128, 130, 132, 135, 139 (left), 149, 170, 178, 186

Melissa Lucas: 161

Scott McBride, © The Taunton Press, Inc.: p. 136

Todd Meier, © The Taunton Press, Inc.: p. 13, 106

Kerry Ann Moore, © The Taunton Press, Inc.: p. 167 (left)

Courtesy National Garden Bureau Inc.: p. 80 (bottom)

Scott Phillips, © The Taunton Press, Inc.: p. 83 (top), 117, 172

Courtesy Rita Randolph: p. 54, 162, 191, 197

Courtesy Rizaniño "Riz" Reyes: p. 45

Courtesy Linda Roark, p. 5 (top), 31

Dennis Schrader: p. 51, 89

Courtesy Jill Schroer: p. 44

Courtesy Sheila Schultz: p. 38

Danielle Sherry, © The Taunton Press, Inc.: p. 10 (left), 28, 32, 34, 39, 43, 50, 70, 86 (top), 88 (left), 95, 102, 157,

Steve Silk: p. 96 (bottom)

Virginia Small, © The Taunton Press, Inc.: p. 14, 118

Brandi Spade, © The Taunton Press, Inc.: p. v, vi (top: center, bottom: center), 3, 8, 9, 12, 15, 16 (left), 17, 18, 23, 24, 26, 29, 33, 35, 37, 53, 57 (right), 58, 71, 76, 81, 82, 90, 94, 103, 116, 119 (design by Carter Lee Clapsadle), 140, 143 (bottom left), 156, 158 (right), 167 (right)

Marc Vassallo, © The Taunton Press, Inc.: p. 193

ILLUSTRATIONS

Krista Borst, © The Taunton Press, Inc.: p. 165

Beverly Colgan: p. 27

Susan Carlson: p. 181

Michael Gellatly: p. 166, 172, 188

Chuck Lockhart, © The Taunton Press, Inc.: p. 159, 175

Index

A

Aeonium, 31, 38
Agaves, 30, 90, 93
Apricot tree, 168
Arrowheads, 98

B

Bamboo teepee, 21
Banana plants, 59, 61, 194
Basil, 20, 32, 50, 80, 85, 154, 182
Baskets, bottomless (as "containers"), 113
Baskets, hanging, 128–35
    adjusting length, 130
    choosing (size and scale), 129, 131
    embellishing, 132
    liner for, 134
    no-care flowers for, 128
    non-flower plants for, 128, 131
    planting tips, 133 (*see also* Potting)
    precautions, 131
    watering tips. *See* Watering
Begonias, 37, 45, 56, 119, 125, 194
Borders, adding depth to, 27
Boxwood, 33, 66
Bugs, good, 189
Bulbs, 163, 195

C

Cabbage, 32, 50, 89
Caring for plants. *See* Fertilizing;
   Overwintering; Pest control; Pruning;
   Watering
Chives, 178, 195
Cleaning pots, 141
Coleus, 9, 16, 17, 46, 53, 55, 61, 121, 124, 184, 194
Color, 41–50
    avoiding potpourri of, 42
    balancing cool/warm tones, 38
    breaking rules of, 39
    coleus for, 46 (*see also* Coleus)
    harmony with, 40, 42
    less is more, 42
    orange-red explosion, 45
    palette for edibles, 50
    of pots, 32, 38–40
    purpleheart for, 47
    red pot example, 32
    by season. *See* Seasons
    silver and gold foliage, 42, 43, 48, 55, 56
    splash of citrus, 44
    straddling both sides of wheel, 49
    variegated potato vine for, 48
    white flowers, 41
Containers. *See* Pots
Contrasting and connecting plants, 17
Copying good ideas, 10
Crotons, 44
Cucumber vines, 88
Cyclamen, 69

D

Deadheading, 186
Depth, adding, 27

Design principles. *See also* Color; Landscape
   design
    adding strong vertical lines, 19
    contrasting and connecting plants, 17
    copying good ideas, 10
    elevating containers, 12, 115
    filling pot to brim, 10
    height considerations, 10, 11, 15, 19, 29
    inanimate objects, 22
    location of edibles, 20
    miniature-plant tips, 12
    multiple pots, 7
    plants complementing pots, 30 (*see also* Pots)
    proportions, 10, 20
    repeating plants, 16
    rule of three, 6
    selecting perennials, 20
    shapes working together, 18
    structure in garden, 20
    texture, 17, 52, 54
    thriller-filler-spiller technique, 6–7
    tradition with a twist, 8
    triangular arrangements, 13
    trying new plants, 9
    using inanimate objects, 22
    vine support, 21
Drama, adding, with plant combinations, 53
Dream Catcher™ beautybush, 55
Drought-tolerant plants, 90–94. *See also*
  Succulents

E

Edibles, 79–89. *See also* Herbs; *specific edibles*
    bold, big pots for, 39
    choosing, 77–78
    early spring medley, 70
    foliage of, 51
    location of, 20
    ornamentals with, 79
    pruning, 179–86
    rearranging plant types, 27
    simple color palette for, 50
    soil for, 152–55
    in tight spots, 88
Elephant ears, 55, 196
Entryways, 15, 24–25
Evergreens, 15, 28, 48, 62, 67, 69, 122, 191

F

Fall plants, 74–76
Fertilizing, 144, 145, 148, 149–52, 154, 155, 194
Fillers, 6, 7
Flower boxes, 125
Flowers
    choosing, 77–78
    deadheading, 186
    edible, 70, 83
    explosion of color, 45
    fertilizing, 149
    fragrant, spring, 69
    layering bulbs, 163
    matching colors to pots, 32

    no-care, for hanging baskets, 128
    pairing with edibles, 50
    perennials, 20
    pruning to optimize, 179, 181
    soil for. *See* Soil
    sowing to optimize, 156
    squirrel-proofing, 189
    summer, 71
    white, for night visibility, 41
Foliage. *See also* Grasses; Plants; Seasons
    big leaves, for big impact, 59
    bright, 62
    complementary, 54
    dramatic, 53
    edible, 51 (*see also* Edibles)
    gold, 42, 48, 55
    shade-friendly, 57, 62, 83, 124
    silver, 42, 43, 56
    texture of, 17, 52, 54
    three-season helichrysum, 58
    trees, 63, 67, 161, 168, 197
Forest-inspired design, 28
Formality, of containers, 34
Fragrant flowers, 69

G

Garlic, 164
Gold foliage, 42, 48, 55
'Goldilocks' creeping Jenny, 6
Grasses, 28, 30, 60–61, 62, 76, 77

H

Hanging plants. *See* Baskets, hanging
Hardening off plants, 159
Hardiness zone map, 198
Height considerations, of plants and pots, 10, 11, 15, 19, 29
Herbs, 27, 80–84, 114, 153–55, 182–85, 190–93. *See also specific herbs*
Heuchera, 9, 67
Hostas, 28, 57, 77

I

'Icicles' helichrysum, 38, 58
Inanimate objects, in designs, 22
Insects, good, 189

J

Japanese sweet flag, 6, 65

L

Landscape design, 23–29
    adding depth to borders, 27
    big plants for big spaces, 29
    forest-inspired design, 28
    front entries, 24–25
    poolside plants, 27
    privacy and screening, 26
    rooftop space, 23
    seating areas, 26
Lemon balm, 195
Lettuce and greens, 20, 70, 72, 79, 85, 114, 188

M

Marigolds, 70, 83
Mint, 32, 82, 83, 176, 184, 185, 192

N

Nasturtiums, 27, 32, 39, 50, 155, 156

O

Orange-red explosion of color, 45
Oregano, 78, 80, 114
Overwintering, 138, 140, 190–97

P

Parrot feather, dwarf, 99
Parrot's beak, 49
Parsley, 50, 51, 70, 155, 191
Peppers, 39, 74, 85, 151
Perennials, 9, 10, 28, 48, 77, 184, 195, 196
Pest control, 187–89
Planting. See Potting; Soil; Watering
Plants. See also Edibles; Foliage; Seasons; Size
   and scale; specific plants
     caring for. See Fertilizing; Overwintering;
       Pest control; Pruning; Watering
     choosing, 20, 77–78
     complementing each other, 54
     complementing pots, 30 (see also Pots)
     contrasting and connecting, 17
     drought-tolerant, 90–94 (see also
       Succulents)
     pinching, to encourage growth, 184
     repeating, 16
     top-heavy, corralling, 40
     for water gardens, 95–99
Poolside plants, 27
Potato vine, variegated, 48. See also Sweet
   potato vines
Potatoes, 166–67
Pot-bound plants, 157
Pots, 30–40
     balancing cool/warm tones, 38
     barrels as, 111
     caring for, 136–41
     chimney-flue liners as, 116
     choosing, 102–09
     cleaning, 141
     color of, 32, 38–40 (see also Color)
     concrete, 40, 103, 107, 112
     consistent look of, 107
     corralling top-heavy plants in, 40
     elevating, 12, 115
     embellishing, 117
     feet protecting, 139
     fiberglass, 67, 106, 107
     filling to brim, 10
     filling voids in, 158–59
     as focal points, 33
     formality of, 34, 102
     heat-durable, 107
     heat-protection tips, 137
     hypertufa, 112–13
     iron, 67, 141
     limestone, 40, 104
     matching to location, 31
     materials and characteristics, 102–09
     mixing styles, 110
     overwintering, 138, 140, 190–97
     plants complementing, 30
     ready-to-go, 78
     simplicity of, 37

     size and scale, 35, 39, 109
     slug-free, 188
     strawberry jars, 114
     tabletop, 36
     terra-cotta, 40, 67, 96, 105, 116, 162
     tiered, 115
     unique or unusual, 37, 110–17
     for water gardens, 96–97
     window boxes, 118–27
     for winter, 107, 140
Potting, 156–68
     apricot trees, 168
     bulbs, 163
     garlic, 164
     gravel, drainage and, 147, 160–61
     hardening off plants, 159
     in large containers, 158–59
     neatly, 157
     opposites together, 157
     tomatoes and potatoes, 164, 165–67
Privacy and screening, 26
Proportion, design principles for, 10, 20
Pruning, 179–86
Purpleheart, 47

R

Rooftop space, selecting plants for, 23
Rosemary, 80, 84, 114, 155, 183, 190–91

S

Sage, 30, 50, 80, 114, 184
Saucers
     as false bottom, 159
     for saving water, 170
Seasons, 64–76
     all-season centerpiece, 64
     fall plants, 74–76
     recycling fall foliage, 75
     spring plants, 69–70
     summer plants, 68, 71–73
     switching plants for interest, 74
     three-season helichrysum, 58
     winter plants, 64–67, 122
Seating areas, 26
Sedums, 31, 38, 40, 68, 74, 77, 90, 92
Shade, plants for, 57, 62, 83, 124
Shrubs, 30, 55, 64, 67, 161, 197
Silver foliage, 42, 43, 56
Size and scale
     big leaves, for big impact, 59
     of hanging baskets, 129
     of plants, 39, 40
     of pots, 35, 39, 109
     tall grass and, 61
     of window boxes, 118
Slugs, controlling, 188
Soil, 144–55. See also Fertilizing; Potting
     for annuals, 145
     checking levels of, 159
     customizing to suit plants, 148, 150
     good additives for, 146
     gravel, drainage and, 147, 160–61
     saving on, in large containers, 158–59
     topdressing, 144
     for vegetables/herbs, 152
     weather determining mix, 148
Spillers, 6, 7, 62, 89, 99
Spring plants, 69–70
Squash, 89
Squirrel-proofing, 189
Structure in garden, 20

Succulents, 38, 90, 92–94, 120, 160
Summer plants, 68, 71–73
Sweet potato vines, 61, 71, 121

T

Tabletop containers, 36
Tarragon, 84, 114
Teepee, for vines, 21
Texture, 17, 52, 54
Three, rule of, 6. See also Triangular
   arrangements
Thriller-filler-spiller technique, 6–7
Thrillers, 6, 7
Thyme, 80, 81, 114, 153, 155
Tiers, 115
Tomatoes, 39, 86–87, 128, 131, 150–51, 164,
   165, 181, 189
Trees in pots, 63, 67, 161, 168, 197
Triangular arrangements of pots, 13
Tropicals, 44, 59, 72, 73, 194, 195

V

Vegetables. See Edibles; specific vegetables
Verbenas, 48, 71, 193
Vines, teepee support for, 21
Vines, types of, 16, 48, 61, 71, 88, 119, 121. See
   also Tomatoes

W

Water gardens/plants, 95–99, 148
Waterfall-like plant, 43
Watering, 169–78
     crystals helping, 172, 173
     drip-irrigation, 176
     hanging baskets, 134–35, 169
     overwatering, 171
     parched containers, 171
     plants requiring minimal water, 177–78
     saving, techniques, 162, 170, 172–73,
       175, 176
     techniques and timing, 169, 174–76
     trickle-down, 175
     wands for, 169
     window boxes, 120, 127
     winter, 196
White flowers, for color at night, 41
Window boxes, 118–27
     adding focus, 119
     air flow/water drainage for, 126, 127
     for curb appeal, 125
     hanging, 126
     modular trays for quick changes, 123
     paired, variety in, 121
     placing plants in, 120
     root-depth precaution, 127
     second-story, 120
     in shade, 124
     size of, 119
     watering, 120, 127
     winter, 122
Winter
     containers for, 14, 107
     overwintering, 138, 140, 190–97
     plants, 64–67, 122
     watering, 196

Z

Zebra plant, 93